Contents

a PaRent's guiDe to LeArniNg difficulties

how to help your child

PETER WESTWOOD

ACER Press

First published 2008
by ACER Press, an imprint of
Australian Council *for* Educational Research Ltd
19 Prospect Hill Road, Camberwell, Victoria 3124, Australia

www.acerpress.com.au
sales@acer.edu.au

Edited by Carolyn Glascodine
Cover and text design by Mary Mason
Typeset by Mary Mason
Printed in Australia by Shannon Books

National Library of Australia Cataloguing-in-Publication data:

Author: Westwood, Peter S. (Peter Stuart), 1936–
Title: A parent's guide to learning difficulties :
             how to help your child / author, Peter Westwood.
Publisher: Camberwell, Vic. : ACER Press, 2008.
ISBN: 9780864318404 (pbk.)
Notes: Includes index.
             Bibliography.
Subjects: Learning disabilities.
             Children with disabilities – Education.
             Education.
             Child development.
             Child rearing.
Dewey
Number: 371.9

Preface

This book is written for parents who want to understand more about the learning difficulties experienced by some children. Most parents want to know *why* their child is having difficulties in learning and *what they can do* to help improve the situation. The advice I give here is based not only on my practical experience gained over the years as a teacher, but also on my knowledge of the current research related to effective teaching and learning.

The term 'learning difficulty' is used in this book in a very general way to refer to any persistent problem that a child, adolescent or adult of any ability level may have when learning a particular subject or skill. For example, a young child may have difficulty learning to read, or an older child may have a problem learning to spell accurately, or to complete certain calculations in mathematics. Any child can experience a learning problem at some time.

While the main focus here is on ordinary children in ordinary schools, I have also included introductory information on children with various disabilities. Many of these children now attend ordinary schools and therefore need the same effective teaching in language, literacy and numeracy that others require. I have argued here that the instructional methods needed by children with disabilities are not markedly different from the effective methods that should be used with all children everywhere. The features of effective instruction are described fully in Chapter 6. Where modifications to methods are needed for certain students, I have described those changes.

I hope that the information I have provided will be of practical value to any parent.

My sincere thanks to Carolyn Glascodine for her excellent work in editing the manuscript for publication. My gratitude, as always, to the friendly, helpful and efficient staff at ACER Press.

PETER WESTWOOD

Quiz

TRY THIS QUIZ BEFORE YOU BEGIN

1 Learning problems in children are always due
to a learning disability.   TRUE / FALSE

2 Children are naturally lazy when it comes
to reading school textbooks.   TRUE / FALSE

3 All children with reading problems should be
referred to as 'dyslexic'.   TRUE / FALSE

4 Which of the following are true?
To help my child overcome learning difficulties in reading,
spelling or mathematics I should:
☐ provide support and encouragement at home
☐ put pressure on my child to make him or her work harder
☐ extend homework time every evening until progress is made
☐ give my child more difficult books or maths problems as
  a challenge
☐ indicate to the child how worried you are by his difficulties
☐ show interest in his or her school work
☐ hire a private tutor for after-school coaching
☐ request that the school have your child assessed by a psychologist
☐ take your child to a psychologist yourself
☐ take your child to your family doctor
☐ remove privileges, such as TV time and computer games until
  progress is made
☐ provide rewards each time when school reports are better
☐ all of the above.

5 An important concept in the psychology of learning is 'automaticity'.
What does this term mean?

6 Another important concept is 'motivation'. What does this term mean? How does it influence learning?

7 It is no longer necessary for children to memorise multiplication tables and other number facts because they can use a pocket calculator.   TRUE / FALSE

8 Learning the relationship between letters and the sounds they represent is an essential step in learning to read and spell.   TRUE / FALSE

9 Have you ever found it difficult to learn something new? If so, how did you deal with the problem?

10 Computer programs can be helpful in improving children's basic literacy and numeracy skills. Do you agree? Why?

CHECK YOUR ANSWERS ON PAGE 106.

RESOURCES | **www.acer.edu.au/westwood**

In a book this size it is impossible to write at great length on each topic. With this in mind, at the end of each chapter, I have provided a list of books and online resources that parents can consult if they wish to pursue a particular topic in greater depth.

Parents can access these online resources through direct links at www.acer.edu.au/westwood.

oNe
Confession

My lifelong interest in children's learning difficulties arose out of my own childhood experiences when attending primary schools in England in the 1940s. At that time I had learning problems, as reflected in my dreadful school reports each term ... 'Unsatisfactory', 'Could do better', 'Lazy in this subject', 'Hope to see improvement next term' ...

My early schooling

By the time I was 10 years of age I am sure that any educational psychologists worth their fee would have labelled me as 'learning disabled' and 'behaviour disordered'. My skills in mathematics were abysmal and my reading ability was far below average. My spelling was atrocious and my handwriting messy and immature in style. A clear indication of my unacceptable behaviour is the fact that at the age of 11, I was expelled from the small private school that I had attended for five years. The teachers there described me as 'rebellious', 'a ring leader', and 'a troublemaker'. I was certainly beyond the control of the two elderly ladies who ran that little school. Unfortunately, the expulsion occurred just before I was due to take the '11+' selection examination – used in Britain at that time to determine a student's future placement in either a grammar school (seen as highly desirable) or a secondary modern school (seen as undesirable).

Naturally, my parents had been very concerned indeed for several years about my poor progress in school; but these were the war years in Britain and my parents were dealing with many other far more pressing and serious matters. Most of the time my father was away, serving in the army, but I can remember occasions when he was home on leave that he would get out the exercise books and go through schoolwork with me.

He was most concerned, I think, with my very poor written work, and he would get me to practise spelling words aloud and then writing the words down several times. The brief sessions of extra tutoring by my father on the rare occasions when he was at home were too infrequent to have any useful impact; and my mother could never get me to persevere with such work when my father was away. Her attempts at doing so always resulted in me throwing a tantrum. Basically, I was not really interested in improving. The fact that I was no good in school did not bother me in the slightest. I was far more interested in roaming the streets and getting into mischief.

As a result of my expulsion from the primary school, I was enrolled in a coeducational state school to complete my final year of primary education. I was in a very large class, with some 35 or more children. This was before the days of seating students together in working groups, and instead we sat in twos at double desks arranged formally in rows facing the blackboard. I remember I was placed next to a boy called Keith, who was successful later in teaching me how to do long division – something that I had not mastered over the previous six years. For the first time since commencing school, I was taught by a male teacher, a Welsh ex-rugby player named Mervyn Jones. Although the war was now over by this time, I think there was still a major shortage of male teachers in schools because many had not returned from the war.

My fortunes change

Having Mervyn Jones as my teacher was a major turning point in my school career. He was a very firm but friendly man who used teaching methods that motivated all the children. In particular, he frequently employed what is now termed 'project-based learning' and took the class on field trips to a local farm, the council offices, a shopping centre, the railway station and several other interesting locations. We collected information, interviewed relevant people, made drawings, and took any printed matter such as pamphlets, timetables, price lists and so forth back to school with us. These resources, together with our own notes and drawings, were then used as the basis of many different classroom activities involving mathematics, reading, writing, speaking and listening. I had never, in my previous school years, had an opportunity to participate in such activities, and the experience left a very great impression on me. Indeed, 60 years later I can still remember vivid details of the farm visit and the field trip to the railway station. Thanks to Mr Jones, my attitude towards learning greatly improved.

But Mr Jones did not rely on activity methods alone. He was also highly skilled at instructing the class in new information and in developing new skills. He was clear in his explanations and demonstrations at the blackboard; and when we were working at our desks on tasks that he had set he would circulate among us to check on what we were doing and to help us individually. When he discovered that someone had not understood something he would often tell the student sitting next to him or her to explain the work again. That is how Keith came to teach me to do long division. Many years later, when I looked at the research on what is termed 'teacher effectiveness' I discovered that Mr Jones had embodied every one of the instructional skills that make a teacher effective. I owe him a very great debt.

Mr Jones restored my motivation to learn, but of course I still had significant difficulties with reading, writing, spelling and maths because I had fallen so far behind in previous years. I failed the '11+' selection examination (no surprise there), but my father wrote to the Essex Education Committee and begged that I be given another chance to sit the examination. I think he used the excuse that my education had been seriously disrupted by the war, and again in the final year when I had to change from one school to another. The outcome was that I was granted a second opportunity to take the test, and this time I passed, enabling me to attend Clacton County High School instead of the secondary modern school.

Once I had settled in at the secondary school, my reports each term showed that I steadily increased my grades until in several subjects I was among the top three students. Strangely enough, given my major weaknesses in literacy in the early school years, I was eventually awarded 'top achiever' prize in English for my examination result in the General Certificate of Secondary Education. Even more surprisingly, I managed to pass the examination in mathematics. I put that progress down firstly to the fact that I received excellent teaching from extremely competent teachers in that grammar school, and secondly that I did not lack intelligence and ability, despite my poor achievement in the primary years. I didn't have a learning disability; but at primary school, I had an attitude and motivation problem.

No labels, please

Perhaps the most important thing for me was that I was never labelled 'dyslexic' – or indeed given any other label for that matter – to account for my poor learning in school. If I had been given such a label, I am sure I would have happily performed down to it; it would have given me an excuse to hide behind. My poor progress in school was due entirely to other factors – family disruptions due to the war, absence of my father in the army, poor quality teaching in the early years, a boring curriculum, and a total lack of interest and effort on my part. I count myself extremely lucky that I had an opportunity later to reverse the 'failure cycle' and to achieve at least some of my potential in life.

SCHOOL REPORT

Your son is very interested in many things.
Unfortunately, none of them are even remotely related to the work we do in this school.

Progress: Unsatisfactory. Must try harder.

KEY POINTS FOR PARENTS

So what are the main messages in this true case history? Perhaps they are these:

- When a child does not make good progress in school there is no reason to assume immediately that he or she has some form of learning disability or disorder.
- If a child has no real interest in the schoolwork being presented, he or she will not make much effort to learn.
- The child who is not learning successfully will quickly fall behind classmates in terms of achievement.
- Once a child realises that he or she is not getting good results, the child usually reduces the amount of effort expended on learning.

Many children with learning difficulties become highly skilled at avoiding work they find difficult or unrewarding.

▶ Negative comments from teachers (and perhaps from parents too) do nothing to motivate the child to 'try harder'; instead, the nagging begins to alienate the child from learning activities in school and at home.

▶ Lack of success in schoolwork often leads the child to seek satisfaction in other pursuits, including inappropriate behaviour.

▶ The key to reversing the learning problem is to have an effective teacher who gains children's genuine interest and motivates them to learn. Effective teachers make children feel successful.

▶ In the right learning environment, and when given high-quality teaching and support, virtually all children can learn.

two
External causes of learning difficulty

There are many possible reasons why a child in school may experience difficulties in learning. Often, a single cause can't be identified because learning difficulties commonly arise from some combination of the following adverse influences:

- subject matter (curriculum content) that is too difficult and is above the child's intellectual level or experience
- inadequate, inappropriate or insufficient teaching
- too little time devoted to practice
- distractions in the learning environment
- detrimental attitude or emotional state of the child
- child's inefficient approach to learning
- frequent absences from school
- lack of support from home
- less commonly, a learning difficulty may be associated with a vision or hearing problem
- even less commonly, it is possible that the child has a specific learning disability such as dyslexia.

Some of the factors in this list are associated directly with the child, but others are part of the total learning environment. We will look in more detail first at the environmental (school-related) factors because they are the more common causes of learning failure, and are too often overlooked by parents and teachers.

School curriculum

In schools, the term 'curriculum' describes the content or subject matter of what is to be taught across the age range. Curriculum content includes essential information, concepts, skills, attitudes and values that society believes children should be helped to acquire. Traditionally, the curriculum in school is organised into 'subjects', such as mathematics, geography, English, French, science, and so forth; although in pre-schools and some primary schools these subjects may be fully integrated, rather than taught separately.

Generally, the content of the curriculum at any particular age is chosen to match the mental maturity level of the children, and to build on their existing knowledge and experience. This is done to avoid creating learning difficulties by introducing a particular concept that is too far beyond the current understanding of average children of that age. For example, we don't try to teach children in the first year of school how to multiply fractions, and we don't require them to critique the plays of Shakespeare; such things are rightly covered much later in school life. In other words, curriculum content (subject matter) is usually organised into what educators call a 'developmental sequence' that progresses smoothly from simple concepts and skills in the early years to more advanced material later.

School curriculum as a source of learning difficulty

The curriculum can become a source of difficulty when the following problems arise: the work is too difficult, the work is boring, or progress is not monitored carefully by the teacher. Let us examine each of these potential problem areas.

The work is too difficult

For some reason, a teacher might decide to ignore the normal developmental sequence embodied in any well designed program, and instead introduce information, concepts or principles that are beyond the level of understanding of some children. A similar problem is created if the teacher progresses too quickly through the curriculum, moving on to new work before some of the children have mastered earlier topics or skills. This can happen if the teacher is inexperienced, inefficient, or perhaps is teaching a new subject for the first time.

Even when teachers do follow the recommended curriculum sequence, in fairly large classes with students of varying ability, it is not surprising that from time to time some children are given work that is either much too complex, or much too simple – both situations leading to frustration and disengagement. When the demands of curriculum content and learning activities are pitched too high or too low, learners may cease to learn.[1]

In an ideal situation, the content of the school curriculum should be challenging enough to motivate the children, but not so challenging that it causes some children to become confused and discouraged. If subject matter is unavoidably complex, the teacher should break the material down into smaller steps and teach that content very carefully, checking frequently for understanding. 'Nothing recedes like success' if the subject matter gets too difficult too quickly.

The work is boring

Ideally, children need to be genuinely interested in what they are required to learn and they need to perceive the topic or skill as being of value to them. While it is certainly possible to learn things that do not interest you, it is far easier to maintain attention and give maximum effort to learning if the material is genuinely interesting. Psychologists refer to such material as 'intrinsically motivating'. In contrast, dull material causes boredom, and boredom leads to off-task behaviour such as daydreaming and time wasting. Once the child's attention is lost, no useful learning occurs and over time the child begins to have problems with this school subject.

It is true, of course, that not all curriculum content can be intrinsically motivating. For example, practising addition and subtraction processes in arithmetic in order to become fast and accurate is not necessarily intensely interesting. In such cases, we may need to present this work in novel ways, through games and activities or computer software; and we may need to reward and praise children from time to time for engaging willingly in such work.

---

1   Paas, F., Renkl, A., & Sweller, J. (2004). Cognitive load theory: instructional implications of the interaction between information structures and cognitive architecture. *Instructional Science, 32*, 1–8.

Children's progress is not monitored carefully

One important aspect of the curriculum involves the regular assessment of children's learning. This is usually achieved through some form of testing, together with careful observation and checking of children's work in exercise books or folders. The main aim of such testing and observation is to reveal any children who are not doing well and who may need further instruction and additional practice. If teachers do not regularly check on children's progress, they may not notice quickly enough when a particular child is having difficulties. If the learning problem is not recognised early and remedied, it is likely to get worse.

Sometimes there is the problem that even if a teacher does assess children regularly he or she never has time later to help those who reveal their difficulties. Over the years we have tried to ensure that teachers understand that 'assessment must lead to action' – but in reality this often does not happen through lack of time and resources in school.

Teaching method as a source of difficulty

The term 'teaching method' refers to the way in which a teacher presents new topics to the children, engages them in appropriate learning activities and provides corrective feedback. Methods range from formal (for example, directly presenting and explaining new information or demonstrating a new skill to the children) to the informal (for example, creating a situation in which children are required to discover new information through their own activities). A single lesson in any subject may involve some direct teaching, some student activity using instructional materials, some group discussion, and some feedback and summarising by the teacher.

Teaching methods are usually described as tending towards either 'teacher-directedness' or 'student-centredness' in their emphasis. Different subject areas in the school curriculum call for different methods of teaching in order to achieve the goals for learning in that subject. Teachers need to select the most appropriate teaching methods to suit the type of subject matter to be taught, the age and ability level of the children, the children's previous experience and knowledge, and the available time and resources.

Until recently, the method of teaching was rarely investigated as a possible cause of learning difficulty. Teachers seem to assume that if something is taught (which usually means explained or demonstrated), it is automatically learned; and if it is not learned, then the problem must be due to inadequacies in the child's own ability, motivation or persistence, not to the effectiveness of the teaching method.[2] Parents also assume too readily that a learning problem must be related directly to the child's ability or effort, not to the method of instruction. Researchers in the field of education are now recognising, however, that learning problems arise if inappropriate methods of instruction are applied. Not all methods are equally effective in achieving particular goals in learning. Let us examine the teaching of reading and mathematics as examples of situations where some popular approaches have proved to be less effective than others.

Direct teaching versus indirect teaching: the case of learning to read

In the past few years, important reports[3] published in Britain, the United States of America and Australia have been highly critical of the way in which literacy skills are being taught in the majority of primary schools in those countries. Basically, the reports indicate that over the previous two decades the direct teaching of *phonic skills* – designed to enable a young child to read and spell using knowledge of letter-to-sound correspondences – has been seriously neglected. Instead, teachers have been trained and encouraged to use a popular method called 'whole language approach' in which direct teaching of phonic skills and spelling is frowned upon. Teachers who use whole language approach believe that children will learn to read, write and spell without needing direct instruction if they are given daily opportunities to engage in reading and writing activities, and if they receive positive feedback from the teacher. In other words, these teachers believe that learning to read and write is a 'natural' process; all it requires is for children to be self-motivated and active learners in order to discover

---

2   Nuthall, G. (2004). Relating classroom teaching to student learning: A critical analysis of why research has failed to bridge the theory–practice gap. *Harvard Education Review, 74*, 273–306.

3   House of Commons Education and Skills Committee (Britain). (2005). *Teaching children to read*. London: TSO; National Reading Panel (US). (2000). *Teaching children to read: An evidence-based assessment of the scientific research literature on reading and its implications for reading instruction*. Washington, DC: National Institute of Child Health and Human Development; Rose, J. (2005). *Independent review of the teaching of early reading: Interim report*. London: Department for Education and Skills; Department of Education, Science and Training (Australia). (2005). *Teaching reading: National inquiry into the teaching of literacy*. Canberra: Australian Government Publishing Service.

their way to functional literacy with minimal guidance from the teacher. The evidence is, however, that some children (particularly in the early stages) simply do not discover the basic principles of reading and writing in an alphabetic language unless they are clearly and directly taught. The absence of direct teaching is the main cause of reading difficulty for most of these children.

Direct teaching versus indirect teaching: the case of mathematics

In recent years, the teaching of number skills and mathematical problem solving has also favoured a 'discovery' or 'activity' approach rather than direct instruction. It has become unpopular, for example, for teachers to drill children in basic arithmetic processes and multiplication tables because it is claimed that they will easily pick up these skills along the way if they simply engage every day in solving problems that involve counting, measuring, comparing and calculating. But some (possibly many) children do not benefit from this activity-based approach[4] and instead need to have basic numeracy skills taught directly and then practised to the point of mastery. This issue will be discussed in more detail in a later chapter. It is clear that some children have significant difficulties learning mathematics because the underlying skills and concepts have not been taught clearly and effectively or practised sufficiently.

Problems associated with discovery and inquiry-based learning

While it is true that active methods such as discovery learning and inquiry-based learning are often quite effective in arousing children's interest and in holding their attention, it is equally true that these methods are not particularly effective when first introducing children to a new subject or skill. It is much more effective to begin by teaching children new information and skills directly, rather than expecting them to discover these for themselves by trial and error. Even in subjects such as science, where discovery and inquiry have been most strongly promoted, it is

---

4   Kirschner, P. A., Sweller, J., & Clark, R. E. (2006). Why minimal guidance during instruction does not work: An analysis of the failure of constructivist, discovery, problem-based, experiential and inquiry-based teaching. *Educational Psychologist, 4, 2,* 75–86.

now believed that direct teaching is often much more effective.[5] If the children are first taught the information and skills they need for particular situations, discovery and inquiry activities are much more valuable later. Unfortunately, that is not the way in which these methods are usually applied in schools.

Children who lack confidence in their own ability, and who may have poor literacy, numeracy and study skills are often totally at sea in unstructured learning situations; they may look busy, but they learn and remember very little. Unstructured learning situations can create problems in learning.

Other problems associated with teaching

The following factors associated with teaching can also cause or exacerbate learning difficulties:

- The teacher, when explaining, instructing or questioning, may use language that is too complex. Children quickly learn not to listen if they do not understand what the teacher is saying – thus creating problems in learning. As teachers gain experience, they usually become more skilled in effective classroom communication.
- There may be a shortage of suitable teaching materials (books, diagrams, computer programs, maps, etc). In areas such as literacy development, for example, the provision of sufficient books and other print material at the correct level of difficulty greatly enhances children's opportunities to learn.[6]
- Due to pressure from an overloaded curriculum, or for other reasons, the teacher may move ahead too quickly and devote too little time for practice. As we will see later, abundant successful practice is one of the surest ways of learning effectively and developing essential skills. Practice is also essential for overcoming learning difficulties if they do arise.
- Sometimes children experience difficulties in concentrating in classrooms that are noisy or where different activities are going on at the same time. Activity methods tend to create a number of distractions that some children can't ignore.

---

5   See Adelson, R. (2004). Instruction versus exploration in science learning. *Monitor on Psychology, 35*, 6. Online at: http://www.apa.org/monitor/jun04/instruct.html

6   Tse, S. K., Lam, J. W., Lam R. Y. H., Loh, E. K. Y., & Westwood, P. S. (2007). Pedagogical correlates of reading comprehension in English and Chinese. *L1 Educational Studies in Language and Literature, 7, 2,* 71–91.

 Associated with classroom activities and cooperative methods is the practice of seating children in working groups around tables. Such grouping can create a very distracting situation where individual children in the group find it hard to attend to and complete their own work due to the activity of others.

 In addition, group work can create a classroom management problem for the teacher, and he or she may have difficulty monitoring children's work closely enough to recognise when certain individuals are having difficulties. If the difficulties are not detected, no extra support will be provided and the problems accumulate. The experts suggest that teachers should address this problem by setting different levels of work for different ability groups or individuals within the class. Schools now refer to this practice as 'differentiation' or 'adaptive teaching'. In reality, it is far from easy for teachers to present work at a variety of levels within the same classroom, at the same time giving high-quality instruction and support to individuals. The larger the class, the more difficult it is to differentiate the curriculum effectively. Regardless of all the publicity that differentiation receives in curriculum guidelines for teachers, differentiation is actually extremely difficult to plan, implement and sustain every day.

RESOURCES | www.acer.edu.au/westwood

Useful books on learning difficulties include:

Bender, W. (2008). *Learning disabilities: Characteristics, identification and teaching strategies* (6th ed.). Boston: Pearson–Allyn & Bacon.

Knight, B. A., & Scott, W. (2004). *Learning difficulties: Multiple perspectives*. Frenchs Forest, NSW: Pearson Educational Australia.

Westwood, P. (2004). *Learning and learning difficulties*. Melbourne: Australian Council *for* Educational Research.

General information on learning difficulties can be located online at:

http://www.bupa.co.uk/members/asp/tng/parents/learning/
http://www.dest.gov.au/sectors/school_education/publications_resources/
    other_publications/successful_programs_strategies_for_children.htm
http://www.hellofriend.org/learning/difficulties.html

KEY POINTS FOR PARENTS

▶ Learning difficulties may be caused when subject matter in the curriculum is too difficult relative to the child's current ability and knowledge.

▶ When subject matter is boring (that is, not intrinsically motivating) children may still need to master it; so it is necessary sometimes to provide extra encouragement and rewards (extrinsic motivation) for persisting with the work and making an effort.

▶ Different teaching methods are not all equally effective. Some currently popular methods can create problems for some students.

▶ Most children do best if they receive direct teaching when first beginning new areas of learning such as reading, writing, spelling or maths.

▶ Direct teaching in the early stages enables children to develop essential knowledge and skills to use successfully in other less directed learning situations.

▶ Talk to your child and your child's teacher to find out how basic literacy and numeracy skills are taught in the school.

▶ Ask what provisions are made in the school to assist children who are having difficulties in learning.

threE
Causes associated with the child

Despite the factors within the school curriculum and teaching approach that can cause difficulties in learning, summarised in Chapter 2, it seems that most teachers, psychologists and researchers still tend to focus almost exclusively on so–called 'deficits' or weaknesses within the child to account for learning problems. Even parents tend to assume immediately that there is something 'wrong' with their child if school progress is unsatisfactory. So, it is necessary for us now to examine factors associated with the child that can also cause problems in learning.

Detrimental attitude or emotional state

Almost all children first enter school with a positive attitude. They are generally keen to take part in classroom activities and they expect to be successful when attempting everything the teacher asks them to do. However, it doesn't take long for some children to experience failure or personal inadequacy. Perhaps something they try to do does not work out well – a drawing turns out badly and other children laugh at it; or when asked to write the numeral 12 on the board the child writes it as 21, again resulting in embarrassment. The child is quick to realise that if he or she stops drawing pictures and avoids being called upon to write on the board, the chances of being ridiculed are greatly reduced. This is the beginning of the well-known 'failure syndrome' in which the child, through fear of getting something wrong, avoids participating fully in important learning activities, and thus begins to fall behind other children through passivity and lack of practice. Some children will try to protect their feeling of self-worth by refusing to attempt any task the teacher sets for them. They would rather be thought of as naughty and disobedient than run the risk of revealing that they can't do the work.

The effect of failure on a child's confidence and motivation can be devastating. It must be acknowledged that failure is not a pleasing experience, and given sufficient exposure to it almost any student will develop avoidance strategies. From a child's point of view, the basic message of the 'failure syndrome' is that, 'If at first you don't succeed, maybe you will *never* succeed'. The 'failure syndrome' probably accounts for many instances of ongoing learning difficulties and avoidance behaviour across all school subjects. The effects of early failure are cumulative.

Constant failure can lead to the state called 'learned helplessness', in which the child comes to believe that he or she is incapable of succeeding with anything new the teacher introduces. The child cannot conceive of being able to succeed through personal effort and has to rely instead on strong support from others. This encourages the child to become passive and dependent rather than active in learning situations. Learned helplessness greatly impairs motivation and participation.

Learning difficulties can also be caused if a child is distracted by anxiety about some aspect of family life, such as arguing between parents, fear of parental separation, illness or financial problems. Other worries may relate to friendship difficulties within the peer group. This type of worrying or anxiety can prevent a child from concentrating in class.

Frequent absences from school

If children are often absent from school due to ill health or for other reasons, they may miss out on important new work that is being presented in class. Loss of continuity and the creation of gaps in the learning of a school subject can often lead to problems. Frequent absences can have a detrimental effect on almost all school subjects, but mathematics seems to be most at risk because it relies on each new concept and skill being built on a firm foundation of earlier concepts and skills.

Absence from school can also mean that a child does not have the same opportunity to develop and maintain effective study habits compared to children who are always present and have acquired appropriate routines for learning. Becoming an effective learner requires good study habits and routines.

Child's inefficient approach to learning

Children who learn easily have usually acquired effective ways of going about the work that teachers set for them. We say that such children have developed good 'learning strategies' and efficient 'task-approach skills'. For example, if the teacher asks the group to write a story about a wizard and a black cat, the children may use the strategy of jotting down some ideas and a few key words on rough paper first, and then numbering the ideas in an effective sequence to use in the story before starting to write. They also know how to seek help and advice from the teacher when necessary, and how to check and revise their work. If asked to solve a problem in mathematics, these children approach the task step by step, asking themselves relevant questions as they go, and checking at each step. In contrast, children who have learning difficulties may simply look at the problem and give up or quickly guess an answer or copy the solution from another child. Much more will be said later about the importance of teaching all children effective strategies to use when attempting classroom tasks.

Specific learning disability

Specific learning disability (SpLD) is a term applied by psychologists to approximately two or three children in every 100 whose learning difficulties cannot be traced back to any lack of intelligence, problems with vision or hearing, or insufficient teaching. This small group of learners has ongoing difficulty in mastering basic skills of literacy and numeracy. The experts tell us that SpLD can impair the ability to learn to read (dyslexia), to spell (dysorthographia), to write (dysgraphia), to perform mathematical calculations (dyscalculia), or to recall words, symbols and names quickly from memory (dysnomia). Some children with SpLD also have problems with social relationships – difficulty in making and retaining friends – and a few have minor difficulties with physical skills and coordination.

It is generally true that the difficulties of children with a learning disability are not recognised early enough in school, and many of these children are considered simply to be lazy or uncooperative. In most countries, the method for identifying children with SpLD is for an educational psychologist to assess the child's level of intelligence using an intelligence test, and then to obtain accurate measures of ability in reading, spelling and mathematics. Any marked difference between level of intelligence (IQ) and level of attainment in these skills suggests significant 'under-achievement' and might indicate the presence of a learning disability.

The most widely recognised learning disability is *dyslexia*. Dyslexia is often defined as a 'disorder' causing difficulty in learning to read despite normal instruction, adequate intelligence and opportunity to learn. This form of reading problem is thought to be present in approximately 2 per cent of the school population, although some reports suggest a higher figure. The oral reading performance of dyslexic students tends to be very slow and laboured, with great mental effort having to be devoted to the identification of each individual word. Comprehension of what has been read is therefore usually very poor. The child tires easily and avoids the frustrating task of reading.

A child with dyslexia typically exhibits the following problems:

▶ Difficulty in analysing spoken words into separate sounds. This difficulty then causes major problems with learning phonics and spelling.[1]

▶ Difficulty in recalling words from memory or quickly naming familiar objects.[2] This difficulty in rapid recall then causes major problems in building a memory bank of words recognised immediately by sight, and in remembering letter-to-sound correspondences.

▶ Difficulty in making adequate use of the meaning of a sentence to assist with word recognition (teachers refer to this as a weakness in 'using contextual cues').

▶ Inability to develop adequate speed and fluency in reading.

▶ Weakness in understanding what has been read.

▶ Perception problems occur in some cases, resulting in frequent reversal of letters and numerals. A few children report distortion or blurring of print when reading.

In addition, many children with dyslexia also exhibit:

▶ hyperactivity and attention problems

▶ inefficient learning strategies

---

1   Muter, V., & Snowling, C. (2004). *Early reading development and dyslexia.* London: Whurr.

2   Vukovic, R. K., & Siegel, L. S. (2006). The double-deficit hypothesis: a comprehensive analysis of the evidence. *Journal of Learning Disabilities, 39, 1,* 25–47.

- emotional, motivational and behavioural problems due to persistent failure
- learned helplessness, anxiety and depression
- negative attitudes towards reading, writing and mathematics, and towards school in general.

In many cases of dyslexia, as in other types of learning difficulty, the children do not appear to have developed an effective system for approaching tasks such as phonic decoding, reading for meaning or writing a story. Their inefficient approach produces a high error-rate and much frustration. It has become popular in recent years to say that these children need to 'learn how to learn' so that they can tackle activities like reading and writing with a greater chance of success. The important thing to note here is that the current evidence suggests that children can be taught to use more efficient learning strategies; this will be discussed in practical terms later.

Dyslexia remains a controversial topic. While some experts argue strongly that dyslexia is quite different from any other form of reading difficulty, others regard it as simply a variation of the same problem. Reading disability has attracted an enormous amount of research interest over the past 50 years, but it is quite clear that this has not resulted in any major breakthrough in special teaching methods or instructional resources. It is difficult to visualise that any teaching method found useful for children with general problems in learning to read would not also be highly relevant for other children identified as dyslexic – and vice versa. If we examine the literature on teaching methods for children with SpLD,[3] we usually find a range of valuable teaching strategies that would be helpful to all children.

Any child with a learning problem requires assistance, and there seems little to be gained from seeking to differentiate between SpLD and 'non-SpLD' students; the need for high-quality, effective instruction is equally strong in both groups. But maybe parents feel more comfort in having their child classified as 'dyslexic' rather than 'a weak reader'. All children who find learning to read and write difficult are best served by designing and delivering intensive high-quality instruction, rather than by identifying them with a label.

---

3   Lerner, J., & Kline, F. (2006). *Learning disabilities and related disorders* (10th ed.). Boston: Houghton Mifflin; Lewis, R. B., & Doorlag, D. H. (2006). *Teaching special students in general education classrooms* (7th ed.). Upper Saddle River, NJ: Pearson-Merrill-Prentice Hall; Pierangelo, R., & Giuliani, G. (2006). *Learning disabilities: A practical approach to foundations, assessment, diagnosis and teaching*. Boston, MA: Pearson-Allyn & Bacon.

Attention Deficit (Hyperactivity) Disorder

A condition that has gained much publicity in the past decade is *attention deficit disorder* (ADD). Some children who have this disorder are also hyperactive, so the new term *attention deficit hyperactivity disorder* (ADHD) was coined to categorise this group.

Children with ADD and ADHD have learning difficulties that are not related to lack of intelligence or to inadequate teaching. Their inability to concentrate and control their level of random activity has a very detrimental effect on their school progress.[4] They are often in trouble because their behaviour is disruptive in class. They seem not to be able to learn from the adverse consequences of such behaviour and still tend to respond impulsively and inappropriately (they 'act without thinking') in a variety of situations even after being disciplined by teacher or parent. Their schoolwork is often unfinished or contains many careless errors. They rarely listen when spoken to or reasoned with directly. They have trouble organising themselves and their belongings, and they have a poor ability to manage their time and meet deadlines. Children with hyperactivity always seem to be restless, unable to remain in their seat for long, and are easily distracted. They are often noisy and talkative. Some children with ADHD show defiant behaviour towards authority figures and socially aggressive behaviour towards other children.

Genuine cases of ADHD can only be diagnosed by trained professionals who will test the child using a number of measures and will carry out observation of his or her behaviour. It is sometimes argued that too many children are given the ADHD label inappropriately;[5] that is, their negative behaviour is not due to any disorder but to outside influences such as lack of firm discipline at home or over-stimulation by electronic and other media. However, the evidence suggests that some 5 per cent of children do have a serious problem in attending to learning tasks and in controlling their own impulses which is unrelated to behaviour management at home. Research studies have shown that the best management results with these children are obtained by using a combination of medication, behaviour modification and personal counselling.

---

4   Wright, C. (2006). ADHD in the classroom. *Special Education Perspectives, 15, 2*, 3–8.

5   Timimi, S. (2006). A critique of the international consensus statement on ADHD. In Slife, B. (Ed.) *Taking sides: Clashing views on psychological issues* (14th ed., pp. 210–213). Dubuque, IA: McGraw-Hill.

In the home situation, it is important to establish some simple rules and routines that should then be consistently followed. Try to provide a distraction-free area for the child to use when doing homework. Homework should be done at a set time each day, with the opportunity to take short breaks within that period if necessary. Help the child plan ahead for each school day and have all materials ready for each lesson. The child may need to carry a 'daily plan + reminders' card in his or her pocket or school bag. Try always to give directions to the child in simple, concise statements; don't overload them with information. The child should repeat important information back to you. Parents must work very closely indeed with school staff so that careful plans to change the child's behaviour are maintained consistently and reinforced in both home and school settings.

More information on ADHD and its identification and management can be obtained from the sources listed below.

RESOURCES | www.acer.edu.au/westwood

Useful books on general learning difficulties include:

http://www.dest.gov.au/sectors/school_education/publications_resources/
    schooling_issues_digest/schooling_issues_digest_learning_difficulties.htm

Information on specific learning disabilities can be located online at:

http://www.helpguide.org/mental/learning_disabilities.htm

Information on attention deficit hyperactivity disorder can be located online at:

http://www.cdc.gov/ncbddd/adhd/symptom.htm
http://www.netdoctor.co.uk/diseases/facts/adhd.htm

KEY POINTS FOR PARENTS

▶ Children who begin to experience learning difficulties in school often develop negative attitudes towards learning. This adds to their problem.

>>

▶ Regardless of the original cause of a learning problem, it is usually the child's emotional reactions to it that maintain and worsen the problem over time.

▶ Constant worry or anxiety impairs a child's ability to concentrate in school.

▶ The only way out of the 'failure syndrome' is to provide a child with many more opportunities to be successful and to recognise personal progress.

▶ For some children, it is necessary to present new information and skills in smaller steps, with much repetition and guided practice at each step – not always easy for the busy classroom teacher to provide for an individual because there are many other students in the class also needing supervision.

▶ Some children do not approach learning in a systematic manner and therefore need to be taught more effective strategies (plans of action) for tackling schoolwork.

▶ Specific learning disability is a possible – but relatively uncommon – cause of a child's learning problem; other causes are more likely.

▶ Giving a child the label 'dyslexic' does absolutely nothing to help reduce his or her learning difficulties.

▶ Children with any form of learning problem all benefit from intensive, high-quality instruction.

four
Intellectual disability and autism

Children with general learning difficulties (estimated to be about 16 per cent of the school population) and with specific learning disability (2–3 per cent) comprise together the largest number of children with special educational needs in our schools.[1] There are, however, other children who experience difficulty in learning and in gaining normal access to the school curriculum. These children may have physical disabilities, impaired vision, impaired hearing, autism or intellectual disability. Others may have emotional or behavioural disorders.

Until fairly recently, children with these disabilities or problems were almost always placed in special schools or special classes because it was believed that their learning difficulties would prevent them from making much progress in ordinary schools. It was felt that a special school provided an opportunity to offer children with disabilities a curriculum and teaching approach that more appropriately met their needs. In the past decade, however, there has been a worldwide endeavour to place many of these children in ordinary schools, rather than in special schools; and to try to make the regular educational programs offered in ordinary schools more 'inclusive' of all children. As a result, the number of children with special educational needs in ordinary schools has increased. In most developed countries, special schools now accommodate only those children with the most severe degrees of disability or impairment.

---

1   Westwood, P. S., & Graham, L. (2000). How many children with special needs in regular classes? *Australian Journal of Learning Disabilities, 5, 3,* 24–35.

Placement – a dilemma for parents

For parents of children with a disability, it is often extremely difficult to decide whether or not to have their child educated in an ordinary school or in a special school. Obviously, parents want their child to have the best opportunity to learn, not only in terms of knowledge and skills within the curriculum but also in terms of social adjustment and independence in the community. Many parents therefore prefer an ordinary school placement because they believe their child will benefit greatly from being with other children who are learning normally and displaying reasonably normal behaviour. But in making the decision concerning appropriate placement, parents have to consider:

- the degree to which their child is handicapped by his or her disability
- the extent to which their child can function independently
- the child's own wishes concerning schooling
- the quality and quantity of special support that the ordinary school can provide
- the quality of the program offered in the special school.

It is often difficult to get accurate information on the quality of support in a school – ordinary or special. It is not unusual for schools to describe their special education support and their inclusive curriculum in fairly glowing terms, but the reality of the situation sometimes turns out to be rather different. It is absolutely true that some children with disabilities have been integrated into ordinary schools very successfully. Many schools are operating programs that are indeed inclusive, and the teachers are managing to provide good quality education for children across a wide ability range. However, it is equally true that some children with special needs have been placed in ordinary schools without adequate support. Many teachers in these schools feel inadequately trained to teach these children and to meet their needs within the ordinary classroom. All parents are advised to seek as much information as possible about the special education support that is promised in a school. It is helpful to be able to talk with other parents who already have a child with special needs at that school, to hear their opinion. It is obviously also helpful to talk with the teacher or teachers who will be most involved with your child's program. Ask them to describe in detail how the child will be assisted. Ask how you can best assist the child at home in order to supplement the school program.

Almost all schools now encourage a much closer relationship with parents than was the case some years ago. For example, if a child has a special educational need, most schools now begin to address this need by drawing up an *individual education plan* (IEP) for the child. This plan will establish some clear goals covering personal, social and academic development to provide a focus for teaching and behaviour management over the next few months. Parents are required to be involved in establishing the IEP so that they are aware of exactly what the school is intending to do, and how they will do it. Parents are also able to provide valuable input to this process because they know their child well. The IEP can be used as a yardstick against which to measure progress and improvement over time.

Let us now look a little more closely at the areas of disability that may cause a child to have special educational needs. The following pages are not intended to provide an in-depth coverage of various disabilities but rather to provide a brief introduction. Parents requiring more information are referred to the books and resources listed later.

Children with intellectual disability

Other than the population of children with general learning problems already discussed, students with intellectual disability represent the next largest group of students with special educational needs. For an individual to be identified as having an intellectual disability, he or she will obtain a measured intelligence quotient (IQ)[2] below 70 and has limitations in reasoning and in independent functioning. The most obvious characteristic of individuals with intellectual disability is that they experience significant difficulty learning almost everything that others can learn with ease. Children with intellectual disability usually appear to be much less mature than their age peers, tending to exhibit behaviour that is typical of younger children. Their behaviour patterns, skills and general knowledge are related more closely to their mental age than to their chronological age. They can and will learn if provided with an appropriate instructional program, adequate support, and teaching methods suited to their level of ability. The extent to which major changes in teaching approach are required depends upon the degree of intellectual impairment, ranging from mild to severe.

---

2   The average IQ in the population is 100, with 130 and above regarded as high intelligence.

Children with *mild* intellectual disability tend to be very similar to children who have been described in the past as 'slower learners'. Most children with mild intellectual disability attend ordinary schools now and receive additional support in that setting. To assist these children, their teachers usually try to simplify learning activities and the content of the curriculum where necessary. The children may also attend additional remedial classes in the school.

Children with *moderate to severe* intellectual disability are more commonly accommodated in special schools or special classes. Many children with severe intellectual disability also have additional handicaps or problems (physical, sensory, emotional, behavioural) and are frequently described as having 'high support needs'.

For some children with disabilities, a special education setting may still offer the best environment to meet their needs. The purpose of having special schools and special classes was – and still is – to create a situation in which curriculum content, resources, and methods of instruction can be geared appropriately to the students' needs and abilities. Classes are also smaller in special schools, allowing more opportunity to work with individuals.

Areas of difficulty

General development: Intellectual disability often results in significant limitations in development in the following areas. These areas are priorities within the curriculum and IEP for children with intellectual disability:

- self-care and daily living skills
- language and communication
- social skills
- literacy and numeracy
- self-regulation
- independent functioning in the community.

Attention: Children with intellectual disability often appear to have major problems in paying attention in a learning situation and are easily distracted. A teacher needs to think of many ways of helping the child focus on a learning task and maintain concentration. Without adequate attention, any child will fail to learn what the teacher is trying to teach.

Memory: Many students with intellectual disability also have great difficulty retaining information in their long-term memory. This problem may be linked with the failure to attend closely to the learning task, as discussed above. The memory weakness indicates that a greater amount of repetition and practice is required with these children to ensure that information and skills are mastered and remembered. Frequent revision of previous work is also needed. It is claimed that once these children do eventually get something stored firmly in their memory, they can recall that skill or information as well as any other child.

Generalisation: In learning theory, 'generalisation' means that a learner is able to use information or skills outside the situation in which they were first taught. It is typical of many children with intellectual disability that they learn a particular skill or concept in one place with one teacher but then fail to transfer that learning to a different situation. The message from this is that skills and concepts must be taught and rehearsed in many different contexts.

Language: One of the main characteristics of children with intellectual disability is the very slow rate at which many of them acquire speech and language. Even the child with mild disability is likely to be somewhat behind in language development. Some individuals with severe and multiple disabilities never develop speech. So, for them, alternative methods of communication may need to be developed; for example, sign language or picture communication systems.[3] Many children with intellectual disability require the services of a speech therapist; but even then, may continue to have language problems.

Language ability is important in life because it serves the following functions:

▶ It enables the child to make his or her needs, opinions and ideas known to others.

▶ Concepts are more effectively stored in their memory if they have a representation in words.

▶ Language is the main medium through which school learning is conducted.

---

3 Heller, K. W., & Bigge, J. L. (2005). Augmentative and alternative communication. In S. J. Best, K. W. Heller, & J. L. Bigge (Eds.) *Teaching individuals with physical or multiple disabilities* (5th ed.). Upper Saddle River, NJ: Pearson-Merrill-Prentice Hall.

▶ Positive social interaction with others is heavily dependent upon effective language skills.

▶ Language is important for regulating behaviour.

For these reasons, development of language and communication skills in children with intellectual disability is given high priority in the special school curriculum.

Social development: Children with intellectual disability often experience difficulty making friends and gaining social acceptance among other children – particularly if they have certain irritating or troublesome behaviours. Some children with intellectual disability are rejected by other children because of their irritating behaviour rather than because they are disabled. Inappropriate behaviour such as aggression, shouting or temper tantrums makes it difficult for a few of these children to be socially accepted. If the child with a disability is to make friends and be accepted in the peer group, these negative behaviours must be eliminated and social skills training provided.

Teaching approaches for children with intellectual disability

It is essential that teaching and learning situations for children with intellectual disability are *reality-based* – 'learning by doing'. To acquire new knowledge and skills, these children need to experience things actively at first hand. If children with intellectual disability are to learn important number skills, for example, they should learn them not only from maths books, computer games and instructional materials, but also from real situations such as shopping, stocktaking, measuring, estimating, counting, grouping, recording data and comparing quantities.[4] Similarly, reading skills should be developed and practised using a variety of resources such as instruction cards, recipes, brochures, magazines and comics, as well as through books, games and flashcards. More will be said on reading in Chapter 7.

Children with intellectual disability also need direct teaching, with curriculum content broken down into very simple steps to ensure high

---

4   Xin, Y. P., Grasso, J.C., Dipipi-Hoy, C. M., & Jitendra, A. (2005). The effects of purchasing skill instruction for individuals with developmental disabilities: A meta-analysis. *Exceptional Children, 71, 4,* 379–400.

success rates. Lessons that employ direct instruction use an active style of teaching that gets many successful responses from the children in the time available and makes much use of reinforcement. The method ensures that children master important concepts and skills before moving on. There is heavy emphasis on practice, but lessons are made enjoyable and entertaining. It has been found that direct instruction is extremely effective for students with disabilities, particularly for teaching basic skills.[5] Direct instruction is among the most extensively researched teaching methods and has consistently proved more effective than child-centred approaches for introducing the beginning steps of basic academic skills.[6]

Other basic principles to consider when working with children with intellectual disability include the following:

▶ Do not sell the children short by expecting too little from them.
▶ Provide frequent guidance and prompts to enable a child to manage the steps in a new learning task.
▶ Gradually reduce the amount of guidance so that the child becomes more independent.
▶ Frequently assess the learning that has taken place against the child's objectives in the curriculum (IEP).

RESOURCES www.acer.edu.au/westwood

Useful books on intellectual disability include:

Heward, W. L. (2006). *Exceptional children* (8th ed.). Upper Saddle River, NJ: Merrill-Prentice Hall.
Turnbull, A., Turnbull, R., & Wehmeyer, M. L. (2007). *Exceptional lives: Special education in today's schools* (5th ed.). Upper Saddle River, NJ: Pearson-Merrill-Prentice Hall.

>>

5   Turnbull, A., Turnbull, R., & Wehmeyer, M. L. (2007). *Exceptional lives: Special education in today's schools* (5th ed.). Upper Saddle River, NJ: Pearson-Merrill-Prentice Hall.
6   Carnine, D. W., Silbert, J., Kameenui, E. J., Tarver, S. G., & Jongjohann, K. (2006). *Teaching struggling and at-risk readers: A direct instruction approach.* Upper Saddle River, NJ: Pearson-Merrill-Prentice Hall.

General explanations of intellectual and developmental disability can be found online at:

http://en.wikipedia.org/wiki/Intellectual_disability
http://www.eumap.org/topics/inteldis/reports/summaries/uk/uk.pdf

For recommendations on teaching approaches and school provision, see:

http://www.aph.gov.au/Senate/committee/eet_ctte/completed_inquiries/
　　2002-04/ed_students_withdisabilities/submissions/sub157a.doc

Children with autism

Approximately six or seven children in every 1000 display some degree of autism.[7] Individuals with the condition vary greatly one from another. Some children with mild autism are close to normal in many aspects of their behaviour, but others are very low-functioning in terms of intelligence, self-control, communication and social skills. Some children with severe degrees of autism often sit for hours engaged in odd repetitive habits such as flapping their fingers in front of their eyes, and a few engage in self-injurious behaviour such as biting or scratching at their own arms.

Areas of difficulty

Autism is a form of developmental disability in which the most obvious characteristics are:

- lack of a normal emotional relationship with others
- impairment of communication
- reduced ability to learn, particularly through observation and by imitation
- the presence of repetitive behaviour patterns (e.g. rocking, hand flapping)
- obsessive rituals, and the desire to preserve 'sameness' in surroundings and routines
- lack of imaginative and creative play.

7　'CDC releases new data on the prevalence of autism'. Johns Hopkins Bloomberg School of Public Health. Online at: http://www.jhsph.edu/publichealthnews/articles/2007/lee_autism. html

Children with autism are among the most difficult students to place successfully in regular classrooms. Those with severe autism are usually functioning at a level too low to cope with the demands of even an adapted curriculum. As many as three-quarters of children with autistic disorders have IQ scores well below 70, and ongoing special education is required to address their learning needs. In Australasia, the United States of America and Britain, only about 12 per cent of children with autism receive their education in ordinary schools. However, most of the higher-functioning students, including those with *Asperger Syndrome*, do attend mainstream schools. Individuals with Asperger Syndrome have some of the behavioural and social difficulties associated with other degrees of autism, but they tend to have intelligence and language skills in the average or even above average range.

Teaching and management approaches for autism

Many different approaches have been used to reduce the negative behaviour often associated with autism, including drug treatment, diet control, therapy, behaviour modification and self-management training. Of these approaches, behaviour modification has produced the best results.[8] Behaviour modification involves the setting of clear objectives for teaching compliant behaviour and eliminating inappropriate behaviour through direct teaching and positive reinforcement.

Many other approaches have been tried, including sensory-integration training, music therapy, play therapy, facilitated communication, speech and language training, and social skills coaching. A recent technique that appears helpful in developing autistic children's awareness of 'normal' codes of behaviour is the use of 'social stories'. Social stories are simple narratives, personalised to suit the child's own needs and behaviour, to which the child can relate. The theme and context of the story help the autistic child interpret and respond more appropriately to typical social situations; for example, sharing a toy, taking turns or standing in line.[9]

---

8   Dempsey, I., & Foreman, P. (2001). A review of educational approaches for individuals with autism. *International Journal of Disability, Development and Education, 48*, 103–16.

9   For information on social stories see Crozier, S., & Sileo, N. M. (2005). Encouraging positive behaviour with social stories. *Teaching Exceptional Children, 37, 6*, 26–31.

There is general agreement that the focus of any support program should attempt to:

- stimulate intellectual development
- encourage language and communication
- promote social development.

The following priorities should be set when working with autistic children:

- Be consistent in your management of the child (firmness plus affection).
- Gain the child's attention, and speak clearly and simply to aid comprehension.
- Build up the child's attention span.
- Challenge the child just enough to encourage progress towards new goals.
- Extend what you are teaching into different situations (for example, at home, out shopping, travelling on the bus).
- As far as possible, ignore attention-seeking behaviour and reward appropriate and compliant behaviour.
- For autistic children who lack speech, the use of visual cues (hand signing, pointing, picture cards, symbols) is usually necessary in most teaching situations.

Teaching sessions for children with autism generally need to be implemented according to a regular schedule. Objectives are best achieved by using both direct instruction methods and by using the natural opportunities that occur during the child's daily life. Evidence has proved that the most effective teaching programs are *highly structured* and *delivered with intensity*. New information, skills or behaviour need to be taught in small steps, using consistent and direct methods. All teachers, parents and other caregivers must know the objectives of the teaching and management program, and must work together to ensure consistency. It is essential that parents are trained in any special teaching or management techniques that are needed because the child spends more time at home than at school. Sewell[10] writes, 'Remember – everything you teach children with autism to do for themselves will be one more skill they will not have to depend on someone else to do for them the rest of their lives.'

---

10 Sewell, K. (2000) *Breakthroughs: How to reach students with autism*, Verona, WI: Attainment Company.

RESOURCES www.acer.edu.au/westwood

Several school-and-family approaches have been devised for autistic children, including a program called TEACCH (Treatment and Education of Autistic and Communication-handicapped Children) and *SCERTS* (Social Communication, Emotional Regulation and Transactional Support). A description of these programs is beyond the scope of this book, but information can be located online at:

http://www.teacch.com/whatis.html
http://www.barryprizant.com/scerts_model.htm

General information on autistic spectrum disorders can be located at:

http://www.nimh.nih.gov/publicat/autism.cfm

A summary and critique of treatment and management methods is available online at:

http://www.mousetrial.com/links_treatments.html

KEY POINTS FOR PARENTS

▶ Children with intellectual disability will learn, but usually at a slower rate than other children.
▶ These children need teaching that is clear and direct, with much practice and frequent application in real-life situations.
▶ More practice than usual is required in learning new information and skills in order to overcome memory and attention difficulties.
▶ Social skills may need to be taught to some children who have problems in relating to other children.
▶ Behaviour modification and direct instruction have proved to be most effective for children with autism.
▶ Parents need to work closely with school staff to ensure that learning from school is reinforced and maintained in the home and in the community.

fivE
Impaired vision, impaired hearing, physical disability

In general, physical and sensory impairments account for a very much smaller number of children with special educational needs, compared to those with intellectual disabilities. Some children with impaired sight or hearing or physical disabilities will be of average or better than average intelligence. Many of these children can cope well with the ordinary school curriculum if they are provided with necessary *access and support*. Some of this support comes in the form of assistive technology to help them operate effectively in the school environment and access instructional resources.

Children with impaired vision

Impaired vision can obviously contribute to learning difficulties. While blindness affects a relatively small number of children, it is important to remember that less severe vision problems occur as an *additional* handicap in many other forms of disability. For example, many individuals with cerebral palsy also have serious problems with vision, as do many with traumatic brain injury or intellectual disability.

When a child is described as 'vision impaired' it does not necessarily mean that he or she is blind; it means that the child has a serious sight defect that cannot be corrected simply by wearing spectacles. Among children with impaired vision there are those who are totally blind and those who possess varying degrees of partial sight.

Areas of difficulty

There are at least three areas in which blind children and those with seriously impaired vision may need to be taught additional skills. These areas are mobility, orientation and the use of Braille.

Mobility: Blind students, and those with very limited sight, need to be taught *mobility skills* to enable them to move safely in the environment. Increased mobility adds significantly to the quality of life for persons with impaired vision and helps them to gain access to a wider range of learning experiences. Mobility skills include *self-protection techniques* (for example, when moving in unfamiliar places, holding the hand and forearm in front of the face for protection while trailing the other hand along a wall or rail); *using sounds* to locate objects and events in the environment (for example, identifying the position of a construction site; recognising the noise of approaching traffic; locating voices); and moving with the aid of a *long cane* to warn of potential hazards.

Orientation is the term used to describe how a blind person becomes familiar with a particular environment (for example, the classroom, the route from school to home) and at any time knows his or her own position in relation to objects such as furniture, barriers, open doors or steps. Developing mobility and orientation are two of the primary goals in helping blind students towards increased independence. Without these skills, the learning opportunities for a blind person are seriously restricted.

Braille, the system using patterns of tiny raised dots to represent words and numbers that can be read by fingertip touch, is of tremendous value to persons who lack sight. It provides an alternative method of communication for children who are blind or whose remaining vision does not enable them to read enlarged print. If a child's intelligence is adequate, the younger he or she begins to learn Braille, the better. However, Braille is a difficult code to learn, so its use with students who are well below average intelligence is not always successful.

Assistive technology

The use of assistive technology can be of enormous help to children with partial sight. Many devices have been designed to enable a student to cope with print. Equipment includes magnification aids, CC television (used to enlarge an image), calculators and electronic dictionaries with speech output, 'compressed speech' recorders, and equipment to reproduce Braille pages or embossed pictures, diagrams and maps.

Some students with impaired vision benefit from 'low tech' aids such as modified desks with raised tops to bring materials closer to the child's eyes, or with a lamp attachment for increased illumination of the page. Some forms of vision impairment respond well to brighter illumination, but in other conditions, very bright light is actually undesirable. The specialist who is aware of the student's vision problem will be able to give advice on illumination level.

Teaching children with impaired vision

It is essential to hold positive expectations for the progress of all children with impaired vision, and to provide them with many new challenges. A problem with vision should not exclude a child from access to the normal curriculum, although many modifications may need to be made in how material is presented and how the child responds. Appropriate modifications for teaching at home include:

▶ reading aloud all written instructions to ensure that the child understands the work

▶ using very clear descriptions and explanations when teaching; vivid verbal explanation has to compensate for what the child cannot see

▶ making sure that any assistive equipment is always at hand and in good order

▶ ensuring that your own writing is neat and clear, using larger script than usual

▶ avoiding overload of worksheets with too much information and density of print

▶ allowing partially sighted students to use a thick black-ink pen to produce larger writing

▶ preparing exercise papers with darker ruled lines

▶ using a photocopier to enlarge print to 24 or even 48 point

▶ allowing much more time for students with impaired vision to complete their work.

RESOURCES   **www.acer.edu.au/westwood**

Useful books on vision impairment include:

Bishop, V. E. (2004). *Teaching visually impaired children* (3rd ed.). Springfield, IL: C.C. Thomas.

Barraga,N., & Erin, J. (2001). *Visual impairments and learning* (4th ed.).
Austin, TX: Pro-Ed.

Information on vision impairment can be located online at:

http://www.tsbvi.edu/Education/corecurric.htm
http://www.viguide.com/
http://www.bbc.co.uk/cbeebies/grownups/special_needs/blind/teacherann/

Children with impaired hearing

Children are referred to as *deaf* if they are unable to interpret the speech
of others or if their own speech is distorted. Children who can hear some
sounds, and can therefore make some use of their remaining hearing, are
termed *hard of hearing* or *partially hearing*. Many children with impaired
hearing have no other disability; but it is important to note that hearing
impairment is often present as an additional disability in children with
intellectual disability, cerebral palsy or language disorder.

There are two main types of hearing loss, *conductive* and *sensori-neural*.
Each type presents its own set of difficulties. For example, the use of a
hearing aid may significantly help an individual with conductive hearing
loss, but may not improve hearing in the case of a sensori-neural loss.

Conductive hearing loss: Conductive loss occurs when sounds are not
reaching the middle or the inner ear because of some physical blockage to
or damage to the ear canal or the eardrum. Common causes are a build-up
of wax in the ear canal, a ruptured eardrum, infections in the middle ear
or damage to the tiny bones in the middle ear.

Sensori-neural loss: This problem is related to the inner ear or to the
auditory nerve. The most serious hearing losses are often of this type. As
well as being unable to hear some sounds, even those that are heard may be
much distorted. It is reported that in some cases individuals with sensori-
neural loss are very sensitive to loud noises, perceiving them to be painfully
loud. This problem of distortion means that wearing a hearing aid may
not always help because making a distorted sound louder does not make it
any clearer.

Areas of difficulty

An inability to hear places a young child at serious risk of delay in many important areas, including the acquisition of vocabulary, speech and literacy skills. Social development may also be disrupted. It is said that deaf children's lack of vocabulary (knowledge of words and their meanings) limits their understanding of what is talked about in the classroom and slows down their ability to learn to read and spell. A priority goal in their education is therefore to advance their language skills as much as possible. Any improvement in language will allow each child to understand much more of the curriculum, make better use of his or her intellectual potential, and develop socially. Over the past two decades, the movement towards integration of children with disabilities into ordinary schools has emphasised the value of including hearing-impaired children in ordinary classes. It is believed that regular class placement increases the need and motivation for deaf children to communicate. These children will experience better social interaction and will be exposed to the more accurate language models of other children.

Speech: The speech of children with impaired hearing tends to develop later than normal and, depending on the degree of deafness, often has very poor rhythm and phrasing together with a flat and monotonous tone of voice. Speech therapy and 'auditory training' are often required. Active parental involvement at home is also essential for stimulating speech and language development.

Reading: Typically, children with significant hearing loss tend to fall several years behind the average level in terms of reading ability as they progress through primary school. This reading lag has a negative impact on their performance in all subjects across the curriculum. Many of their difficulties in reading and spelling are thought to stem from their problem in perceiving speech sounds accurately. This problem results in difficulty in learning phonic skills that are necessary for decoding words in print (see Chapter 7). From the time the child enters school a high priority must be given to direct and intensive teaching of reading. While the beginning stages of instruction for hearing impaired children can focus more on building a sight vocabulary by visual methods rather than by phonics, later the teaching of phonic skills and word analysis will be essential if the child is to become an adequate reader. Suitable activities for vocabulary building and phonics are described in Chapter 7.

Writing: The written expression of deaf children is often problematic, with grammar and vocabulary the major weaknesses. The children's difficulties include inaccurate sentence structure, incorrect order of words (for example, 'She got black hair long', instead of 'She has long black hair'), incorrect verb tense, difficulties representing plurals correctly and inconsistencies in using correct pronouns. The written work of older deaf students has many of the characteristics of the writing of much younger children.

Spelling: Spelling instruction needs to be systematic rather than incidental. For deaf children, attention will need to be given to the development of visual memory to enable them to spell and check words by eye rather than ear. The 'look-say-cover-write-check' strategy is particularly helpful and needs to be taught thoroughly (see Chapter 9).

Assistive technology

Hearing aids: Hearing aids are of various types, including the typical 'behind the ear' or 'in the ear' aid, and the more recent radio frequency (FM) aids. An audiologist assesses the specific needs of the child and a hearing aid is prescribed to suit the individual's profile. While they are very helpful to children with a conductive hearing loss, no hearing aid fully restores hearing, even when carefully tailored to the child's characteristics. The great limitation of the commonly used hearing aid is that it amplifies all sound, including noise in the classroom. The advantage of the radio frequency aid is that it allows the teacher's voice to be received with minimum interference from environmental noise. The teacher wears a small microphone and the child's hearing aid receives the sounds in the same way that a radio receives a broadcast transmission. The child can be anywhere in the classroom or the school yard, and does not need to be close to or facing the teacher, as with the conventional aid.

Cochlear implants: Cochlear implants are normally recommended only for children who are profoundly deaf and cannot benefit at all from other forms of hearing aid. A cochlear implant is a device used to electrically stimulate the auditory nerve. Many developed countries are now carrying out the surgery required to implant this form of assistive device at a very young age. While the child can begin to perceive the electrical stimulation soon after surgery, it normally takes at least a year for any gains in the child's language skills to become evident. Many children with cochlear implants still need ongoing support from sign language to understand fully what is said.

Teaching children with impaired hearing

Teachers, tutors and parents must consider the following principles when working with children with hearing loss:

▶ Make greater use of visual methods of presenting information.

▶ Use clear and simple language when explaining new concepts.

▶ Teach new words thoroughly.

▶ Write new vocabulary on the board. Ensure the child hears the word, sees the word and says the word.

▶ Revise new vocabulary regularly.

▶ Repeat instructions clearly while facing the child.

▶ Don't give instructions while there is noise in the room.

▶ Where possible, write instructions in short statements on the board, as well as giving them orally.

▶ Attract the child's attention when you are about to ask a question or give information.

▶ Check frequently that the child is on task and has understood what he or she is required to do.

▶ Make sure you involve the deaf child in the lesson as much as possible.

▶ Don't talk while facing the board; a deaf child needs to see your mouth and expression.

▶ Try to reduce background noise when listening activities are conducted.

▶ Check that the hearing aid is working; a child won't always tell you when a battery needs replacing or a connection is broken.

RESOURCES **www.acer.edu.au/westwood**

Useful books on hearing impairment include:

Stewart, D. A., & Kluwin, T. N. (2001). *Teaching deaf and hard of hearing students: Content, strategies and curriculum.* Boston, MA: Allyn & Bacon.

Mahshie, J. J. (2006). *Enhancing communication skills of deaf and hard-of-hearing children in the mainstream.* Clifton Park, NY: Thomson-Delmar.

Information available online at:

http://www.as.wvu.edu/~scidis/hearing.html
http://www.shef.ac.uk/disability/teaching/hearing/5_strategies.html
http://www.teachersfirst.com/sped/prof/deaf/education.html

Children with physical disabilities

In the case of children with physical disabilities, their greatest need is often help in accessing normal learning situations. It is important to realise that a physical disability does not automatically impair a child's ability to learn. The intelligence levels for children with physical disabilities cover the full range from gifted to severely intellectually disabled. While it is true that some children with physical impairment do have significant learning problems, one should never make assumptions about an individual's capacity to learn simply on the basis of a physical disability. However, even those physically disabled students with good learning potential may need a great deal of personal support at school. Some students may have a high absence rate due to therapy or treatment appointments during school hours, and frequent health problems. Absence means that the teacher may need to provide the child with appropriate work to do at home, and the parent may have to act as tutor.

Assistive technology (AT) plays an important part in the education of students with physical disabilities by increasing the range of movement, aiding communication, and enabling better access to the curriculum. AT ranges from 'low tech' equipment such as pencil grips, modified scissor grips, slant-top desks, specially designed seating, electric wheelchairs, walking and standing frames, and head-pointers, through to 'high-tech' adaptations such as modified computer keyboards or switching devices that do not require hand movements.

It is beyond the scope of this book to provide details of each physical disability, impairment or health problem. Attention here will be devoted to some brief introductory comments on cerebral palsy, spina bifida and traumatic brain injury.

Cerebral palsy

Cerebral palsy (CP) affects approximately two children in 1000. It is a disorder of posture, muscle tone and movement that results from damage to areas of the brain responsible for controlling movement. The damage occurs before or during birth. CP exists in several forms (for example, spasticity, athetosis, ataxia) and at different levels of severity from mild to severe. Type and severity of the condition are related to the particular areas of the brain that have been damaged, and the extent of that damage. CP is not curable, but its impact on the individual's physical coordination, mobility, learning capacity and communication skills can be reduced through appropriate therapy, assistive technology, training and education.

It is not unusual to find that children with CP also have additional handicaps. At least 10 per cent children with CP also have impaired hearing or vision. Epilepsy is evident in up to 30 per cent of cases of CP and a significant number of the children are on regular medication to control seizures. Medication can often have the effect of reducing individuals' level of alertness, thus creating problems in learning.

AREAS OF DIFFICULTY

Some children with CP tend to lack confidence in their own ability and often develop a rather passive approach to learning, relying on others to do too much for them. In addition to any problems with movement and speech, many children with CP also tend to:

- tire easily and have difficulty attending to tasks such as reading and writing (typing) for more than brief periods of time
- require special physical positioning in order to make best use of their coordinated movements and rely on the parent, teacher or aide to lift and move them.

Academic instruction for children with CP will depend mainly upon their intelligence and motivation. Children with mild cerebral palsy and normal intelligence may simply be slower at completing assignments and therefore need more time. Allowance may need to be made for poorly coordinated handwriting, or the child may be taught to use a word-processor instead. Adapted devices such as pencil grips and page-turners may be required, and papers may need to be taped firmly to the desktop. In special schools, computers with adaptations such as touch screens rather than a keyboard or 'mouse' are useful both for presenting academic work and as a medium for communication with others.

Spina bifida

Spina bifida (SB) is a physical disability resulting from a failure of bones in one part of the spine to close over to protect the spinal cord before birth. The milder forms of SB have no significant influence on learning, and it is estimated that approximately 80 per cent of individuals with the condition have normal intelligence. However, learning difficulties are quite common in the remaining 20 per cent.

AREAS OF DIFFICULTY

In one out of five children with SB, problems are often reported in attention, memory, spatial ability and mathematical skills. In severe cases, lower-body functions are seriously disrupted and the individual may need to use a wheelchair or leg braces. Control of bladder and bowel may be impaired, necessitating the use of a catheter tube to drain urine, a careful diet, and a regular bowel-emptying routine. The management of incontinence presents the greatest social problem for individuals with SB.

Traumatic brain injury

Traumatic brain injury (TBI) refers to acquired brain damage resulting from such events as car accidents, falls, blows to the head, unsuccessful suicide attempts, sports injury, the 'shaken infant syndrome', and recovery after near-drowning. An increasing number of school-age individuals now acquire brain injury from falls, car or sport accidents, and partial drowning.

AREAS OF DIFFICULTY

The effects of TBI on learning can include:

- severe memory problems
- attention difficulties
- slower information processing
- inability to solve everyday problems or plan ahead
- disruption to speech and language
- impairment in walking and balance
- onset of epilepsy

▶ vision problems
▶ severe headaches
▶ unpredictable and irrational moods or behaviour.

Often the abilities of students with TBI improve dramatically in the first year following their injury; but after that, progress is often much slower.[1]
The main challenges for the teacher, tutor or parent are:

▶ keeping instructions clear and simple – not overloading the child with information or tasks
▶ finding ways of maximising the child's attention to a learning task (for example, removing distractions; providing cues)
▶ compensating for poor recall by teaching rehearsal (practice) strategies; keeping reminder notes in a pocket; frequently checking the daily timetable
▶ helping the individual plan ahead, set goals and then work towards them.

RESOURCES   **www.acer.edu.au/westwood**

Useful books on physical disabilities include:

Best, S. J., Heller, K. W., & Bigge, J. L. (Eds.) (2005). *Teaching individuals with physical or multiple disabilities* (5th ed.). Upper Saddle River, NJ: Pearson-Merrill-Prentice Hall.
Orelove, F., Sobsey, D., & Silberman, R. K. (2004). *Educating children with multiple disabilities: a collaborative approach* (4th ed.). Baltimore, MD: Brookes.

Online resources include:

http://specialed.about.com/od/physicaldisabilities/a/physical.htm
http://www.bbc.co.uk/cbeebies/grownups/special_needs/physical_dev/ teacher/
http://www.rochester.edu/ada/st_hand.html

---

1   Hardman, M. L., Drew, C. J., & Egan, W. W. (2005). *Human exceptionality: School, community, and family* (8th ed.). Boston: Pearson–Allyn & Bacon.

KEY POINTS FOR PARENTS

▶ Physical and sensory disabilities do not automatically lead to problems in learning. Many children with these disabilities can do extremely well in school if given support and encouragement.

▶ As a parent of a child with this type of disability, it is important to understand the purpose and functioning of any assistive technology that is used to help your child communicate and learn in school.

▶ A close collaboration between home and school will produce the best learning outcomes for the child.

six
General principles of effective teaching

It could be said that there is nothing really 'special' about special educational methods. Some parents imagine that methods used to teach children with learning difficulties must be very different indeed from the methods used with other children in ordinary classrooms; but this notion is not really correct. Working in school or at home with a child with learning difficulties simply requires that we apply *with greater intensity and precision* what is already known about normally effective instructional methods.

As discussed in Chapter 2, classroom research[1] has indicated that all children tend to learn best when the initial stages of teaching are carefully structured. The structure usually involves:

▶ clear presentation (explanation, demonstration and modelling) by the teacher or tutor
▶ checking that children understand the work
▶ opportunities for children to practise what has been presented, under the guidance of the teacher
▶ immediate positive feedback from the teacher, plus any necessary correction of errors
▶ gradual withdrawal of teacher support as children begin to master the skill or concept
▶ frequent independent practice and application
▶ systematic revision at regular intervals.

---

1   e.g. Polloway, E. A., Patton, J. R., & Serna, L. (2005). *Strategies for teaching learners with special needs* (8th ed.). Upper Saddle River, NJ: Merrill-Prentice Hall; Borich, G. D. (2007). *Effective teaching methods: Research-based practice* (6th ed.). Upper Saddle River, NJ: Merrill-Prentice Hall.

Kindsvatter, Wilen and Ishler[2] have remarked:

> As to which learners benefit most from this systematic approach, research tells us that it is helpful for young children, slower learners, and students of all ages and abilities during the first stages of learning informative material, or material difficult to learn.

Let us look in more detail at each of the components of systematic teaching because they apply as much in effective tutoring at home as they do in teaching a whole class in school.

Ensure clear presentation

The most common cause of confusion for children is lack of clarity in teachers' explanations and demonstrations. This can be the beginning of a learning difficulty.

For effective presentation, teachers and tutors, including parents that are acting as tutors to their children, need to consider the following points:

▶ The first step is to make sure that you have the child's full attention (brain, eyes and ears).

▶ If you are explaining something new, always try to use simple language. If you must use difficult words, because they are essential to the subject matter, make sure that you teach the meaning of those words thoroughly and carefully – and check for understanding.

▶ Try to imagine new subject matter from the eyes of a person who has never studied it before. Make it simple. Don't make assumptions about the child's previous knowledge.

▶ There is always a temptation for teachers/tutors to talk (explain) for too long. This means that the child can't possibly process everything that you say (information overload) so he or she stops listening. If you talk too much, 'no listening = no learning'.

▶ Try to keep the amount you present to small units of information; and ask the child something relevant after each step. This keeps the child engaged and gives you evidence of understanding. A good technique is to ask the child to

---

2   Kindsvatter, R., Wilen, W., & Ishler, M. (1992). *Dynamics of effective teaching* (2nd ed.). New York: Longman (p. 231).

explain the last step back to you: 'OK. What did I say that we needed to do next? Tell me, or show me.'

▶ If you are demonstrating something on paper – for example, how to subtract 29 from 113 – make sure that the child can see clearly what you do at each step. 'Think aloud' as you perform each step of the calculation. Write the problem again, and then ask the child to follow the same steps and explain each step to you.

▶ If you are demonstrating at a board, make sure the child is attending closely and can see clearly what you are doing.

▶ If you are demonstrating a skill such as how to open a file on the computer, think aloud as you carry out each step. Then immediately ask the child to imitate what you did and say what you said, when carrying out the same steps.

▶ Remember, a clear demonstration is usually much more effective than a verbal explanation alone; and often a demonstration accompanied by relevant self-talk at each step can be the most effective presentation of all.

Check for understanding

It is vital that you check for understanding at every step when a child is learning something new. Once the child misunderstands or fails to grasp something, anything you do from that point on becomes confusing and useless. It is difficult for a teacher with a large class to check on the understanding of each and every child, but in a one-to-one home tutoring situation it is very much easier. Understanding is usually checked by observing what the child is doing (for example, in a written exercise), asking the child questions, asking the child to explain or setting an appropriate little test or quiz. One thing that will usually not help at all is to ask, 'Do you understand?' It will simply get a nod of agreement.

Guided practice

The only way that a child will master a new skill or concept is to create situations where he or she must apply the knowledge. In moving towards independence, children must engage in much practice in order to internalise the new area of learning.

In the early stages of practice, the teacher/tutor must check carefully that the child is performing correctly and following the appropriate steps;

problems obviously occur if a child is practising a process incorrectly. The role of the teacher/tutor is to guide the child towards error-free, independent performance.

Feedback and error correction

As children engage in guided practice, the teacher/tutor should offer descriptive praise: 'Well done! Each line is getting neater and neater. Good handwriting' or 'I like the way you are checking the result carefully after you have worked it out'. Descriptive praise is important because it helps the child focus on what he or she is doing correctly. Too often, feedback is critical and negative: 'No! No! Not like that! That is not how I told you to do it. Stop!'

Immediate feedback appears to be far more powerful than delayed feedback. When a child is making errors during guided practice, the teacher needs to re-teach (demonstrate again) the correct process, concept or skill and then watch as the child self-corrects and improves. If a child is making many errors, ask whether the fault lies in the clarity of the instruction that was first given, or whether the practice examples are too difficult.

Gradual withdrawal of support

The longer-term aim, of course, is to ensure that children become fully independent in using and generalising new learning. Guide a child's performance only to the point that he or she can take over control.

It has often been observed that parents and other volunteer helpers are often 'too helpful'. In their endeavours to make sure the child is successful and doesn't meet too many obstacles, they step in too quickly with help, guidance and direction instead of empowering the child to take responsibility.

Independent practice and application

Once the child is reasonably confident with a new skill or concept, he or she needs many opportunities to apply the knowledge without guidance and direction from the teacher/tutor. As we will see below, most basic skills and processes involved in school learning need to be developed to a high degree of *automaticity* – the ability to remember something or to do something without having to think about it – and the only way of achieving this is through a great deal of practice. Learning difficulties begin to occur when a child has too little practice in applying essential skills or concepts before being moved up to the next level of difficulty.

Revision

Effective teaching always respects the fact that individuals tend to forget the things that they are not necessarily applying and practising every day. Frequent revision is therefore required. Successful teachers/tutors take a little time each week to revisit some of the work that has been covered before in order to refresh the child's memory. It is valuable for children to experience the feeling of competence that successful revision can provide. Studies have shown that regular revision and informal testing can dramatically improve children's retention of essential information and skills.[3]

The vital role of practice – mastery, maintenance and automaticity

Practice is an essential component of learning. While a few learning experiences are so vivid that they do not require repetition, most types of learning in school do require practice if the knowledge or skill is to be mastered, applied with ease, and maintained over time.

The main benefit resulting from practice is the development of automaticity. When a child can remember a procedure or item of information automatically, he or she uses much less mental effort when engaged in learning activities. For example, the child whose handwriting or keyboard skills have become highly automatic through practice is much better able to give full attention to the ideas he or she is including in a piece of writing. Similarly, the child who has mastered multiplication tables and other number facts can engage much more efficiently in mathematical problem solving. Some instances of learning difficulty can be traced to lack of automaticity in a basic skill. For example, difficulty in comprehending while reading is

---

3   Dempster, F. N. (1991). Synthesis of research on reviews and tests. *Educational Leadership, 48,* 7, 71–76.

often due to lack of automaticity in word recognition. A reader who lacks automaticity is slow and has to expend such large amounts of concentrated effort on simply trying to unlock the print that there is little effort left to concentrate on meaning. This is a frustrating situation and a reader who is weak in basic skills will try to avoid engaging with print, thereby reducing the time spent on essential practice.

The other major role of routine practice is to ensure that knowledge and skills are maintained over time. If a child does not have to recall specific information regularly, or apply a particular skill frequently, this learning will tend to fade away. As stated earlier, forgetting is a natural feature of learning in humans, but regular practice can help to minimise its effects.

Questioning

Asking children relevant questions related to a learning task is one of the most widely used instructional tactics of teachers and tutors.[4] Questioning helps to keep learners actively involved, focused and motivated; and their responses help the teacher/tutor to assess whether or not they fully understand what is being taught.

Questions can be used before, during and after a period of instruction. Questions asked before teaching are designed to arouse the child's interest and to gain a quick impression of what he or she already knows about the topic of the lesson. Questions asked during instruction help to draw the child's attention to important information as it occurs in the lesson, encourages them to think more deeply, and helps the teacher/tutor probe the child's level of understanding. Questions are asked after instruction to assess overall achievement in that lesson and to identify any misconceptions.

The principles of effective questioning are:

- Keep most of your questions simple and direct. The aim is not to confuse the child with unnecessarily difficult or tricky questions.
- Avoid too many questions that can be answered simply by yes or no.
- Learning is achieved best in situations where children gain confidence in answering questions correctly most of the time.

---

4   Kauchak, D., & Eggen, P. (2007). *Learning and teaching: Research-based methods* (5th ed.). Boston: Allyn & Bacon.

▶ Always allow enough time for the child to think about what has been asked; don't jump in too quickly yourself with an answer.

▶ If a child appears unsure or confused, rephrase the question or provide a hint.

▶ Encourage the child to expand upon an answer sometimes by providing more information.

▶ Praise, comment upon and reinforce good answers.

Reinforcement

When working with children, positive reinforcement (any form of reward) is an important component of effective teaching and learning. Reinforcement is particularly important when working with children who have learning difficulties.

Learning theory suggests that when a particular behaviour or response brings a pleasing result or is positively rewarded, that behaviour or response is strengthened and is then more likely to be repeated. In teaching and tutoring situations, reinforcement may come in the form of praise and a smile from the teacher/tutor, a positive remark written on the child's work, a 'happy face' stamp or sticker, time on a preferred activity (for example, time on a computer game), or on rare occasions even a small gift or token. Such rewards from the teacher/tutor are referred to as 'extrinsic reinforcers' to distinguish them from the intrinsic reinforcement that comes from a personal feeling of satisfaction and success when you know you have done something well.

Extrinsic reinforcement is used a great deal in programs designed to change children's behaviour or to develop communication skills. This is particularly the case, for example, with children who have autism or intellectual disability. But the principle of reinforcing correct responses applies equally in any type of teaching situation with any children. For children with a history of learning difficulty, using reinforcers within the teaching or tutoring program can help them feel more successful. By also recording children's successes visually on some form of progress chart or graph, the child can begin to see that improvement is really being achieved.

In the early weeks of a tutoring program, reinforcers should be used quite frequently to help build motivation and confidence. Gradually, reinforcers should be given less frequently, but never abandoned completely.

Attribution retraining

One of the common observations concerning children with learning problems is that they have very little confidence in their own ability to control learning situations or bring about improvement through their own efforts. Studies have indicated that children with learning difficulties do not necessarily associate their failures with the correct cause. For example, they don't acknowledge that perhaps they completed the work too quickly, did not put in sufficient effort, or did not really listen to the instructions. They are more likely to blame factors outside their own control, such as lack of ability, difficulty of the task, bad luck or the teacher's mood on that day. In particular, they may not appreciate the connection between making greater effort and achieving more frequent success. When children believe that effort will not result in improvement they refrain from putting in effort, and instead settle for the belief that the subject matter is too difficult and that their own ability is inadequate. These feelings have a detrimental impact on motivation. If the expectation of failure is high, it is easier for the child to give up and develop avoidance strategies rather than persist.

So, when children fail in a learning situation they may need help in attributing the failure to the correct cause. *Attribution retraining* attempts to reduce learned helplessness by giving the child a much clearer understanding of the real causes of his or her failures. Attribution training can be included within an effective tutoring program by setting achievable tasks for the child and giving encouragement to complete them. When a satisfactory result is achieved, the teacher/tutor and child discuss the work and together identify how and why the result was good. The child is encouraged to use reinforcing self-talk; for example, 'I copied the diagram carefully. I took my time. It looks very good'; 'I knew what to do because I read the question twice'; 'I listened carefully and I asked myself questions'; 'I didn't get that problem correct because I didn't check the example in the book first. Now I can do it. It's easy!' The main purpose in getting children to verbalise these statements is to change their perception of the cause of their failure in schoolwork. Verbalising in this way helps focus attention on the real relationship between effort and observed outcome.

In most cases, attribution retraining seems to have maximum value when it is combined with direct teaching of effective *learning strategies* necessary for accomplishing particular tasks successfully. Evidence suggests that strategy training does produce definite improvement in learning for children with learning difficulties by making them more effective and confident learners.[5]

Strategy training

Many children with learning difficulties appear to lack effective strategies for learning. They seem not to understand that school tasks can be carried out effectively if they are approached with a suitable plan of action in mind. For example, attempting to solve a problem in mathematics requires: (i) careful reading of the problem (ii) identification of the form of answer that is required (iii) recognition of the relevant numbers to use for calculation (iv) selection of the appropriate calculation process (v) accurate completion of the calculation, and (vi) final checking of the answer. This approach to solving a problem represents a step-by-step application of an effective plan of action. In later chapters the teaching of particular strategies for reading comprehension, writing, spelling and mathematics will be described.

Strategy training involves teaching children to apply effective procedures when approaching and completing a particular task or problem.[6] The teaching involves:

▶ direct instruction in using the strategies through teacher demonstration
▶ imitation by the child
▶ guided practice with feedback
▶ independent practice.

The initial stages of teaching and learning involve the teacher/tutor in 'thinking aloud' (using self-talk) as he or she demonstrates the strategy. A teacher who says: 'Watch and listen. This is how I do it – and this is what I say to myself as I do it', is providing a secure starting point for approaching

5   Swanson, H. L. (2000). What instruction works for students with learning disabilities? In R. Gersten, E. Schiller, & S. Vaughn (Eds.). *Contemporary special education research*. Mahwah, NJ: Erlbaum.

6   O'Brien, C. (2005). Modifying learning strategies for classroom success. *Teaching Exceptional Children Plus, 1*, 3 (n.p). Online at: www.http://escholarship.bc.edu/education/tecplus/vol1/iss3/art3

school tasks. The child is then trained to use similar self-talk as a reminder at each step in the process. The teaching of such verbal self-direction is considered very important in helping children with learning difficulties become better self-regulated. But remember that these children often take much longer than other children to adopt new learning strategies, and the process can take as long as six months. Don't give up too soon.

Tutoring in the home environment

In order to tutor effectively at home, parents should consider the following points:

▶ Try to create a calm, positive and supportive atmosphere for the session. Little of value will be achieved if a child is forced to engage in the session against his or her will. In some homes, tutoring sessions are very unpleasant (and usually unproductive) because the child is totally uncooperative, and the parent becomes annoyed and impatient.

▶ As far as possible, establish a definite routine for the sessions – set a regular starting and finishing time; always use the same room; make sure materials are always ready.

▶ Eliminate distractions such as television or radio playing in the background; brother or sister creating interruptions. Remove toys or other objects from the work table.

▶ Try not to prevent the child from watching a favourite TV program; if you do, this will feel like unfair punishment. Negotiate to have the tutorial before or after the program.

▶ The aim of most tutoring sessions will be to engage the child in additional successful practice of work already presented in school. Working one-to-one with the child allows the parent to give frequent praise, encouragement and immediate corrective feedback. Apply the principles covered in this chapter.

▶ Don't make the session last too long; remember that the child has usually had a full day of schooling already.

▶ Don't make any one activity in the session last too long; remember that human concentration span is limited. Take frequent short breaks; vary the activities.

▶ Be positive. Be encouraging. Be firm, but supportive.

▶ Work closely with the child's teacher.

Useful books on effective learning include:

Coyne, M. D., Kameenui, E., & Carnine, D. W. (2007). *Effective teaching that accommodates diverse learners* (3rd ed.). Upper Saddle River, NJ: Person-Merrill-Prentice Hall.

Kerry, T. (2002). *Explaining and questioning.* Cheltenham: Nelson Thornes.

Mastropieri, M. A., & Scruggs, T. E. (2002). *Effective instruction for special education* (3rd ed.). Austin, TX: Pro-Ed.

Westwood, P. (2006). *Teaching and learning difficulties.* Melbourne: Australian Council for Educational Research.

Wragg, E., & Brown, G. (2001). *Questioning in the primary school.* London: Routledge-Falmer.

Useful information can be located online at:

http://special.edschool.virginia.edu/information/interventions.html
http://specialed.about.com/od/teacherstrategies/a/direct.htm

KEY POINTS FOR PARENTS

- Some subject matter is mastered most easily with direct teaching.
- Some children benefit most from direct teaching.
- Modelling, imitation and practice are powerful teaching tactics that have reasonably wide application.
- 'Thinking aloud' by the teacher or tutor is a powerful way to demonstrate effective task-approach strategies to the child.[7]
- Teaching methods must enable learners to develop automaticity in basic skills.
- Teaching methods must also include abundant opportunities for children to apply and extend higher-order skills and strategies.
- Many learning difficulties are prevented if children are exposed to effective teaching.

7   Dorl, J. (2007). Think aloud! Increase your teaching power. *Young Children, 62, 4,* 101–105.

▶ Research has identified steps in teaching that are associated with effective learning.

▶ These steps are described in this chapter and can be adopted by parents when working with their child at home.

▶ It is vitally important to teach children effective learning strategies so that they experience more success and become more independent in their learning.

sEveN
Learning to read: the early stages

The importance of reading

The ability to read is widely recognised as the key to effective learning in all areas of the school curriculum. Difficulties in learning to read will have a negative impact on a child's learning across all school subjects. Reading skills are also required by adults in order to function successfully in the community. The technological age has made it even more important, not less important, that individuals should possess adequate literacy skills. For these reasons, it is perfectly understandable that parents become extremely concerned if their child does not become a good reader early in his or her school life.

Differences between good readers and poor readers

It is rightly said that children build their reading skills most rapidly and effectively by engaging in a lot of reading. It is certainly true that good readers tend to read a great deal – and are highly motivated to do so. Poor readers, on the other hand, read very little, and they therefore miss out on essential practice. It is an unfortunate fact that the children who most need practice in order to develop automaticity, fluency and confidence in their word-recognition skills are the very children who actually manage to engage in the least amount of reading. They use a variety of ploys to reduce the amount of time they spend with books. This happens because poor readers find reading a very frustrating (and often embarrassing) task, and they will avoid books whenever possible; it simply takes too much of their time and effort to try to make sense of the pages of print. Reading difficulties then have a detrimental influence on the child's self-esteem, confidence and motivation.

What knowledge is necessary for learning to read?

Underpinning the ability to read are important understandings about the nature of written or printed language and how it relates to spoken language. These understandings are usually acquired by most children during the preschool years when they handle books and listen to stories read by a parent, brother, sister or a kindergarten teacher. Marie Clay,[1] a New Zealand expert in literacy instruction, refers to these key understandings as 'concepts about books' and 'concepts about print'. The most important of these concepts include:

▶ understanding that books contain interesting stories, descriptions, reports, pictures and instructions – books can be fun to use

▶ an awareness that people who can read are able to translate the marks on the pages into meaningful language

▶ recognising that stories begin at the front of the book and continue on from page to page – understanding that in English language, print begins at the top of the page and the words are sequenced in lines from left to right down the page

▶ knowing the difference in meaning between the terms 'letter' and 'word' – this is important because often a teacher or parent may ask such questions as, 'What is the first word under the picture?' 'What letter do I need to write next?'; so a child must know the difference between the terms 'letter' and 'word' in order to understand instructions and to avoid confusion.

It is also essential that all beginning readers understand that in English language we use an alphabetic code for writing in which letters and groups of letters represent specific speech sounds in fairly predictable ways. While it is certainly true that some words in English are written without perfect

---

1   Clay, M. M. (1985). *The early detection of reading difficulties.* Auckland: Heinemann.

sound-to-letter correspondences (and are therefore more difficult to decode), it is equally true that at least 80 per cent of words can be decoded wholly or partly by using phonic knowledge. This very important point will be developed in more detail later; here it is important to remark that some children with reading difficulties have not grasped the alphabetic principle and have not recognised the value of using phonic knowledge to help them work out unfamiliar words. Many children with learning difficulties still try to remember words simply by their length and shape; this eventually becomes an impossible task.

There are two main abilities or processes involved in reading. The first is *word recognition*, and the second is *comprehension*. Word recognition involves the accurate identification of the words printed on the page and is the first step towards reading for meaning.

Word recognition

Good readers are able to recognise a word in print very swiftly by one of the following methods:

▸ They may immediately recognise the word because they have seen it many times before and remember it from its overall appearance. We say they know the word 'by sight'; it is now part of their *sight vocabulary.*

▸ They may use knowledge of letter-to-sound correspondences to 'sound out' or 'decode' the word. We refer to this process as *phonic decoding.* The most recent research[2] fully supports the importance of direct teaching of phonic decoding skills early in a child's school life.

▸ They may guess or predict the word from the meaning of the sentence in which it is embedded. We refer to this as '*using contextual cues*'. For example, it is fairly easy to predict the final word in the sentence, 'The woman stepped into the lift and pressed the ___'. Accurate guessing of a word is often increased by giving attention to the first letter or letters appearing in the word. For example, when reading the sentence, 'The girl put the book back on the sh___', the 'sh' in the word 'shelf' helps to eliminate other possibilities such as 'desk' or 'table'. Basic knowledge of phonics makes 'guessing' a word easier.

---

2   e.g., De Lemos, M. M. (2004). Effective strategies for the teaching of reading: What works, and why. In B. A. Knight, & W. Scott (Eds.) *Learning difficulties: Multiple perspectives* (pp. 17–28). Frenchs Forest, NSW: Pearson Education Australia.

Children who are beginning to learn to read do not have many words they know immediately by sight. They have not yet had sufficient experience with reading to build up an extensive 'sight vocabulary' of their own. But that will occur quickly for most children as they gain more and more exposure to print. As they become competent in using phonic knowledge to help decode unfamiliar words, these new words are then added to the child's sight vocabulary and do not need to be decoded the next time they are met.

Developing sight vocabulary

The key to building sight vocabulary is frequent exposure to important words and abundant practice in recognising them, saying them and writing them. Note that the 100 most frequently used words make up about 50 per cent of what we read in any type of book, newspaper, magazine or online text messages. Some of the usual ways of providing additional repetition and overlearning of sight vocabulary are described below.

Graded reading books: Some reading books designed for beginning readers deliberately repeat important words frequently in order to give children maximum practice in their identification. For example:

> This is my house.
> This is my bicycle.
> This is my dog.
> My dog is called 'Patch'.
> My dog runs after my bicycle.
> My dog is in my house.

Unfortunately, books with this type of vocabulary control became very unpopular in schools in the 1980s and 1990s because it was felt that the language they use did not represent natural speech patterns. They were abandoned in favour of using 'real books', presenting interesting stories but without any attempt to control the difficulty level of the text. More recently, there has been a swing back towards vocabulary-controlled books for beginning readers and for older children with reading difficulties who benefit greatly from repetition and predictability in texts.

Flashcard activities: One way in which sight vocabulary can be practised is through activities involving *flashcards*. A flashcard is a card 30 cm x 10 cm on which an important word is printed very clearly using a black marker pen; for example **because** . The word should be written in lower-case letters that are not linked together.

A small set of flashcards containing important words for a particular week or a particular topic can be used in several ways. For example, the teacher or tutor can hold up the word for the child to see and they can practise saying the word together. After four different words have been practised (for example, *house, bicycle, dog, this*), the teacher places the cards side by side on the table and says, 'Give me the word *bicycle*'... 'Very good'. 'Now give me the word *house*'. 'Now give me *dog*', and so forth. The cards are then shuffled and spread out again on the table. The teacher or tutor points to one card and asks, 'What is this word? Say it'. And again, 'What is this word? Say it', and so forth until all words have been practised at least three times. Finally, the teacher or tutor says, 'OK. Take your pencil. Look at this word *house*'. (Remove the card after five seconds). 'Now write the word *house*'. In terms of memory processes, these activities have taken the child from the first level of matching the spoken with the written word, through to the final level of independent recognition and recall.

Word lotto: Some teachers or tutors help children master sight vocabulary by playing word lotto games in small groups. The words to be practised are randomly allocated in sets of about six to eight words per lotto card. The example below provides additional practice with words that are often misread and misspelled. Any other set of words could be used. See Appendix A.

they		when		went
	there		their	
said		which		what

The teacher or tutor has a master set of flashcards containing the full set of words. He or she holds up a flashcard to the group, the children read the word aloud and search for it on their own card. If they have the word, they cover it with a counter. The game continues until the first child covers all the words on his or her card. The child must then uncover each word in turn and read it aloud to the group. If he or she manages to do this correctly, that child is declared the winner. Cards are then exchanged, the flashcards shuffled, and the next game begins.

It is very important to recognise that flashcard activities and games such as word lotto should be regarded only as *supplements* to a child's more extensive practice with reading and writing of meaningful text. Practice of sight vocabulary words is only of value if the child can make use of the learning when reading books and other print media.

RESOURCES	www.acer.edu.au/westwood

Useful books on basic sight vocabulary include:

O'Connor, R. (2007). *Teaching word recognition: Effective strategies for students with learning difficulties.* New York: Guilford Press.

Useful lists of words for the first three years of schooling can be found online at:

http://www.msrossbec.com/sightwords.shtml
http://www.mrsperkins.com/dolch.htm

See also Appendix A.

Teaching phonic skills

Alongside the work on sight vocabulary, it is absolutely essential that children are taught phonic skills to enable them to decode words they have not seen before. But before children can learn phonic skills easily, they must possess what is termed *phonological awareness*. This term refers to the ability to understand that spoken words are made up from a sequence of several separate speech sounds produced in rapid succession. For example, the simple word *book* is made from the separate sounds /b/ + /oo/ + /k/. When saying the word book slowly ('stretching it out') these separate sound units (called *phonemes*) can be heard. To understand the principle of phonic decoding from print, a person has to be able to break spoken words down into their component sounds and know that these sounds can be represented by letters. This process represents one of the most essential skills that beginning readers need to possess.

Many pre-reading games and activities presented to children in kindergarten are designed to help develop an awareness of sounds-within-words. The starting point is usually dividing single-syllable words into two parts, using the initial sound, then the rest of the word. For example, the word 'truck' can be most easily reduced to /tr/ + /uck/, and 'shop' can be reduced to /sh/ + /op/. Teachers call the first sound unit an *onset*. The second part of the word is called the *rime*. Dividing simple words into onset and rime units is very valuable pre-reading experience for young children because it helps them understand the principle of subdividing words.

The second important phonological skill is *sound blending*. This blending process is the reverse of subdividing words. In sound blending, the child puts together a sequence of sounds to pronounce a word. For example, /st/ + /oo/ + /l/ = stool. Sound blending plays a key role when a reader is decoding unfamiliar words in print. Children who have been taught all the common letter-to-sound correspondences and can identify the separate letters and sounds correctly in a word still need to be able to link these sounds together to produce the word. Many activities in pre-school help children to blend sounds; for example, 'I spy with my little eye, a /cl/ –/o/ –/ck/ … or a /fr/ –/o/– /g/ … or a /d/ – /i/ –/sk/ … etc'.

Other phonological skills include being able to recognise when two or more words rhyme (for example, *date, fate, gate, hate, late, mate*). Rhyming helps a child understand that many words that sound similar probably share a letter sequence in common. We will return to this point under the section on word families.

When children are competent at identifying sounds within a spoken word the next step is to teach them common letter-to-sound correspondences. Teaching phonics means teaching learners the precise relationships between letters and sounds, and how to use this knowledge to identify unfamiliar words. The favoured method, in which children build the pronunciation of a word in print by sounding out and blending the letters, is called 'synthetic phonics'. Research evidence[3] very strongly supports direct and systematic instruction in phonic skills soon after the child reaches the age of five. This early start provides a firm foundation on which to build higher-order literacy skills. Children should not be left to discover phonic principles for themselves through incidental learning.

---

3   Coltheart, M., & Prior, M. (2006). Learning to read in Australia. *Australian Journal of Learning Disabilities, 11, 4,* 157–164.

The first stage of teaching phonic knowledge is to teach the common sound associated with each of the 26 letters of the alphabet. This is followed by teaching letter groups such as /ch/, /th/, /sh/, /wh/ (digraphs) and common consonant blends such as /br/, /st/, /cl/, /bl/, /dr/, /fl/, etc. Appendix B contains a useful list of such letter groups. Much valuable experience can be gained by blending these phonic units together to make and spell words. Obviously children must also gain most of their experience in applying phonic knowledge as they read appropriate books at their own level of ability, and as they write their own stories and reports. Much valuable phonic knowledge can be acquired and reinforced from the words children are attempting to write every day.

At this stage, the reading and writing of *word families* can help children become familiar with the groups of letters that are shared by words that sound similar. For example:

/–ill/: *hill, bill, fill, mill, kill, Jill, pill, will, still, chill, thrill*
/–ick/: *kick, lick, nick, pick, sick, tick, wick, thick, trick, stick*
/–each/: *beach, peach, reach, teach, teaching, teacher*
/–ink/: *think, shrink, sink, wink*

Later, as children become more competent in reading, they are able to recognise words very rapidly indeed by using these letter groups that *represent pronounceable parts of words*, instead of decoding each word letter by letter. Indeed, it is now believed that skilled reading actually involves the instant recognition of familiar letter groups such as the above, rather than the recognition of whole words or processing of individual letters.

There are many programs designed to teach phonic knowledge in a systematic way. For example, THRASS[4] is designed to teach children how specific letters and letter–groups represent the 44 phonemes in the English language. Approaches such as THRASS, using direct teaching, are highly appropriate for children with learning difficulties who otherwise remain confused about the fact that the same sound units in English can be represented by different groups of letters (for example, /–ight/ and /–ite/) and how the same letters can sometimes represent different sounds (for example, /ow/ as in *flower* or /ow/ as in *snow*). Another example of a

---

4   Davies, A., & Ritchie, D. (2004). THRASS: *Teaching handwriting, reading and spelling skills.* Chester: THRASS UK.

successful program is *Jolly Phonics*.[5] Jolly Phonics sets out to teach 42 basic sound-to-letter correspondences using a multi-sensory approach.

It must be emphasised here, however, that no teacher ever uses a phonic approach *exclusively*; to do so would be to teach early reading and spelling in the most unnatural and boring way. Valid criticisms have been made of some forms of remedial teaching of reading that err on this side and involve nothing but repetitive drilling of isolated skills. The teaching of phonics needs to be done thoroughly, but as part of a total reading program with an emphasis on reading for enjoyment and for information.

RESOURCES   **www.acer.edu.au/westwood**

Additional information on phonics can be found online at:

http://www.nifl.gov/partnershipforreading/publications/reading_
    first1phonics.html
http://coe.sdsu.edu/people/jmora/PhonicsSequence.htm
http://www.reading.org/resources/issues/positions_phonics.html

---

KEY POINTS FOR PARENTS

▷ Before a child can understand the principles of phonics, it is essential that he or she understands how spoken words can be reduced to a sequence of separate sounds. This understanding is termed 'phonological awareness' or 'phonemic awareness'.

▷ The early stages of learning to read MUST include the teaching of letter-to-sound correspondences (phonics) and how this knowledge can be used to decode words in print.

▷ Not all teachers give adequate attention to the teaching and practice of phonic skills.

▷ Early reading also involves the development of a memory bank of words known immediately by sight.

▷ To become a good reader, a child needs encouragement and opportunity to read frequently.

---

5   Lloyd, S., & Wernham, S. (1995). *Jolly Phonics*. Chigwell: Jolly Learning.

eiGht
Moving on in reading

Children's reading difficulties are made worse if they are trying to use unsuitable books. With apologies to the Three Bears and Goldilocks, books for problem readers should be not too easy, not too difficult, but just right. Remaining with books that are too simple will not advance the child's skills. Attempting to read books that are too difficult will cause frustration and avoidance. Choosing the right books is therefore very important, both in school and for home tutoring.

Selecting appropriate reading material

When helping children with learning difficulties select books to read, teachers or tutors should consider the following points:

- Is the topic of the book meaningful and relevant to the age and interest level of the child?
- Is the book visually attractive and appealing?
- Do the illustrations help to support an understanding of the story?
- Is the language used in the text easy to understand?
- Are there too many unfamiliar words?
- Are the sentences too long and complex?
- For some children, it is necessary also to consider size of print and length of book.

Listening to children read

Although almost all the reading we do in everyday life is actually done silently, there is still value in having a child read aloud to an adult sometimes, as part of any literacy program. Listening to a child read enables a parent to determine the range of skills that the child has already acquired. For example, it is possible to judge whether the child seems to recognise most basic sight words easily, whether he or she makes use of context, whether phonic knowledge is automatically applied to sound out unfamiliar words, whether the child self-corrects when errors are made, and whether the child reads reasonably fluently and with expression.

Sessions of reading aloud are best carried out as a shared reading activity, with child and parent taking it in turns to read. However, the ultimate aim is to help the child become a more independent and confident reader, so the amount of direct help the parent provides should be reduced over time. A tutoring approach called *Pause, Prompt, Praise* (PPP) can be integrated into any session. The procedure involves four steps when the child meets a word in print that he or she does not know:

▶ Pause for about 5 seconds to allow time for the child to identify the word. Don't jump in too quickly and tell the child the word. Wait.

▶ If the child still can't identify the word, provide a prompt (a hint) such as thinking of the meaning of the sentence, and looking at the first two letters in the word; or suggest sounding out the word.

▶ When the child succeeds in identifying the word, praise him or her briefly: 'Well done'.

▶ If after prompting, the child still can't read the word, quickly supply the word, and allow the reading to continue.

RESOURCES   **www.acer.edu.au/westwood**

Additional information on the PPP approach can be found online at:

http://www.schoolparents.canberra.net.au/reading_help.htm
http://www.peta.edu.au/Teaching_resources/Teaching_Tips/page__1559.
   aspx

Developing fluency

Readers only become fluent by engaging in a great deal of reading every day. Fluency depends on the reader having a good sight vocabulary (so that high frequency words are automatically recognised), efficient phonic skills, and the ability to use the meaning of the sentence (context) to help predict any unfamiliar words. Fluency also depends on the reading material being at an appropriate level of difficulty relative to the reader's ability. Children who read very slowly – or much too fast – often comprehend poorly.

One way of improving fluency is to use the procedure called *repeated reading*. The teacher or tutor first reads a passage of text while the child follows in the book. Together, they spend a few moments discussing the meaning of the passage. The child then practises reading the material aloud, with corrective feedback from the teacher or tutor if necessary. The child continues to practise the reading until nearly perfect, and finally records the reading on tape. When the recording is played back the child hears a fluent performance, and this provides an important boost to his or her self-esteem. Repeated reading can be particularly useful for secondary school students with reading difficulties, and it should feature as part of any individual intervention program. Allington[1] states that studies have shown conclusively that '… engaging children in repeated readings of a text is particularly effective in fostering more fluent reading in children strug-gling to develop proficient reading strategies' (p. 73). Repeated reading, if coupled with questioning and discussion before and after reading, can also improve comprehension.

Comprehension

Reading with understanding must be the focus of any literacy program from the very beginning; comprehension is not something that comes *after* learning the mechanics of reading. When parents read stories to a young child in the preschool years they can discuss the material and encourage the child to think about and evaluate the ideas in the story. In shared read-ing activities, children's attention should be devoted to seeking and clarifying meaning, explaining, interpreting and summarising. Ask ques-tions that encourage the child to reflect upon what is read: 'Why did the man in the story act in that way? How do we know the woman was getting angry? What do you think they should do next?'

---

1   Allington, R. L. (2001). *What really matters for struggling readers?* New York: Longman.

Children who are good at comprehending text use a variety of ways to support their understanding. For example, they may *visualise* as they read narrative material; they may *pose questions* to themselves; they may *think about the relevance* of what they are reading; they may *challenge the accuracy* of stated facts; and they *check their own understanding* as they read.

Difficulties with comprehension

Comprehension involves using one's vocabulary knowledge and general experience to build correct meaning as sentences and paragraphs are read. It is obvious that difficulties with comprehension occur if a child is weak at the underlying skill of word identification. Slow and laboured reading prevents easy interpretation of meaning.

In order to improve children's comprehension, it is important to consider the possible underlying difficulties. Sometimes comprehension problems stem from the child's limited vocabulary knowledge or lack of fluency. If a child has difficulty understanding what is read, it is worth devoting more time to discussing word meanings, before, during, and after the child has read a passage of text. There is certainly value sometimes in pre-teaching any difficult vocabulary before the passage is read. It is also important to consider whether the book the child is reading is actually too difficult for him or her.

Improving comprehension

Children's reading comprehension can be improved by engaging them in discussion about the topic of the passage and encouraging them to adopt a thoughtful approach. Comprehension can also be improved by teaching children effective strategies for approaching a passage of text in order to get clear meaning from it.[2] Unfortunately, there is evidence that primary school teachers tend not to give sufficient attention to strategy instruction.[3]

---

2   Boulware-Gooden, R., Carreker, S., Thornhill, A., & Joshi, R. M. (2007). Instruction in metacognitive strategies enhances reading comprehension and vocabulary achievement of Third-Grade students. *Reading Teacher, 61, 1,* 7–77.

3   Parker, M., & Hurry, J. (2007). Teachers' use of questioning and modelling comprehension skills in primary schools. *Educational Review, 59, 3,* 299–314.

One example of a simple reading comprehension strategy for children in upper primary and secondary schools is *PQRS*, in which each letter in the mnemonic signifies a step in the strategy.

The four steps in PQRS are:

P = Preview:
First scan the chapter or paragraph, attending to headings, subheadings, diagrams and illustrations. Gain a general impression of what the text is likely to be about.

Q = Question:
Next, generate some questions in your mind: Ask yourself, 'What do I know already about this subject?' 'What do I hope to find out from reading this material?'

R = Read:
Then read the passage or chapter carefully for information. Read it again if necessary. Ask yourself: 'Do I understand what I am reading?' 'What does this word mean?' 'Do I need to read this section again?' 'What is the main idea in this paragraph?'

S = Summarise:
Finally, state briefly in your own words the key points in the text.

The following principles may also help to strengthen comprehension skill development for all children, not only those with learning difficulties:

- Ensure that the reading material presented is interesting and at an appropriate readability level.
- Always make sure children are aware of the purpose for reading a particular text.
- Apply comprehension strategy training, such as PQRS, to real books; don't rely solely on comprehension exercises for strategy training.
- Prepare children for entry into a new book. Ask: 'What do you think this story is about?' 'What do the illustrations tell us?' 'What does this word mean?' 'Let's read the subheadings before we begin'.
- If there are comprehension questions to be answered, read them together *before* the child reads the story or passage that he or she can enter the material knowing what information to seek.

▶ Use newspapers and magazine articles as the basis for discussion and comprehension activities sometimes. Encourage the use of highlighter pens to focus upon key ideas, important terms or facts to remember.

RESOURCES | **www.acer.edu.au/westwood**

Useful information on comprehension can be found online at:

http://www.readingquest.org/strat/
http://www.manatee.k12.fl.us/sites/elementary/palmasola/
    rcompstrat.htm
http://wilearns.state.wi.us/apps/default.asp?cid=24

Cloze procedure

Some children need additional practice in effective use of context and meaning to support rapid word recognition. *Cloze procedure* is useful for this purpose. The procedure merely requires that certain words in a sentence or paragraph be deleted (usually painted-out with correcting fluid on a photo-copied page, or prepared as a paragraph with gaps on a word processor). Variations on cloze procedure involve leaving the first letter of the deleted word to provide an additional clue; or at the other extreme, deleting several consecutive words, thus requiring the reader to provide a phrase that might be appropriate. Sometimes a list of the missing words (in random order) is provided at the top or bottom of the page to facilitate completion of the exercise.

To implement cloze exercises, ask the reader to read the paragraph and suggest the best word or words to fill each gap. For example:

On Saturday evening Brett was going to a party at his friend's _____. But after lunch that day, Brett was riding his b_____ in the street when he suddenly _____ off. He hit his head hard on the gr_____ and received a very bad cut. When he got _____ his aunt cleaned him up and put a _____ on the cut. He was still feeling _____ in the evening, so he could not _____ to his friend's _____.

RESOURCES   **www.acer.edu.au/westwood**

For more information and examples of cloze procedure, see:

http://olc.spsd.sk.ca/DE/PD/instr/strats/cloze/index.html
http://www.lakemunmor-p.schools.nsw.edu.au/cloze/cloze.htm
http://home.earthlink.net/~eslstudent/read/cloze.html

Improving the reading of children with learning difficulties

To summarise important points made in Chapter 7 and Chapter 8, children with reading difficulties require:

- abundant opportunities to read for pleasure and for information
- systematic teaching of phonic knowledge and word-attack skills
- opportunities to build a sight vocabulary of common words
- successful practice, often using material that has become familiar to the child – frequent successful practice is essential to build skills to a high level of automaticity, and to strengthen the child's confidence
- for beginners, more time to be spent on early reading activities such as phonemic-awareness, flashcards, word-to-picture matching, sentence building, copying and writing
- instruction and guided practice in applying reading comprehension strategies
- improved self-esteem through counselling, praise, encouragement, increased success and recognition of personal progress
- daily instruction, which will achieve much more than twice-weekly intervention
- intervention that not only attempts to improve reading but also focuses on the correction of any negative behaviours, such as poor attention to task or task avoidance which are impairing the child's progress
- texts that are carefully selected to ensure a very high success rate – repetitive and predictable texts are particularly helpful in the early stages
- repeated reading of the same text, which seems to increase fluency and build confidence
- parents or others who can provide additional support and practice outside school hours – this ensures maximum progress.

RESOURCES | **www.acer.edu.au/westwood**

Useful general advice on reading and reading difficulties can be found online at:

http://www.pbs.org/wgbh/misunderstoodminds/readingdiffs.html
http://www.kidsource.com/kidsource/content2/help.overcome.html
http://books.nap.edu/html/prdyc/ch8.html
http://www.aft.org/pubs-reports/american_educator/issues/fall04/reading.
   htm

KEY POINTS FOR PARENTS

▶ If children are to make good progress in reading, it is essential to provide them with interesting books at an appropriate level of difficulty.

▶ Listening to children read aloud not only provides them with practice, it also reveals to parents what skills the child has already developed and where more work is needed.

▶ Helping children develop fluency in reading is important. This fluency will come mainly from regular practice.

▶ Some children have difficulty understanding what they read. This situation can be improved by teaching them effective comprehension strategies, through discussing topics and vocabulary with them, and through encouraging them to think critically about what they read.

ninE
Difficulties with writing and spelling

Of all the literacy skills, writing and spelling cause the most problems for children with learning difficulties. Competence in writing relies heavily on vocabulary knowledge and an awareness of English sentence structures, together with skills for planning, composing and revising written language. Spelling requires not only an adequate grasp of phonic principles and knowledge of word meanings, but also good visual memory and proofreading skills.

Writing

Many children with learning difficulties experience no satisfaction at all from writing and will try to avoid tasks involving writing. As we know, avoidance reduces the opportunity to practise, and lack of practice results in no improvement. The child loses confidence and self-esteem, and develops a negative attitude.

Areas of difficulty

Children with learning difficulties often display the following weaknesses:

- limited ability in planning, composing and revising written work
- difficulties in generating and organising interesting ideas
- a tendency to spend no time thinking carefully before writing
- poor ability to impose logical sequence and structure in what they write
- slow and untidy handwriting
- many spelling errors
- limited output of writing in the available time
- no enjoyment in writing; avoidance.

75

Fortunately, the evidence suggests that children can improve their writing skills significantly if they talk through their ideas for the topic before writing begins, and if direct guidance is provided by the teacher during the composing and revising process.[1] With children who lack confidence in writing, structure the task very carefully at each stage, for example, by writing down key vocabulary and some sentence beginnings for the child to use, and reading these together before the child begins to work. During feedback stages do not correct a child's work too harshly but rather encourage the child by offering constructive suggestions.

Too many children with learning difficulties believe that when they write they must have everything correct from the start. Even highly proficient writers never manage to do that. Children need to be introduced to the notion that good writing goes through several draft stages on the way to correctness. In the words of Nicolini[2], writers need to 'get it down before they get it right'.

Teaching approaches

There are two main ways to teach writing. The first has a focus on teaching basic skills and strategies. This skills–based approach uses a great deal of direct instruction from the teacher/tutor. Step-by-step demonstrations are given, showing how to plan, write and edit different forms of text (for example, stories, descriptions, reports, letters). Children then apply what the teacher has demonstrated as they write on topics set by the teacher/tutor. Follow-up vocabulary or grammar exercises are often used. The second approach places emphasis on the process of 'free' writing, encouraging children to experiment by writing in their own way, with basic skills covered incidentally in the form of comments and corrective feedback on their work.

The skills–based approach became unpopular in the 1990s because it is believed to be less motivating for children than encouraging them to write freely on topics they have chosen for themselves. There is also some doubt that skills taught in routine vocabulary and grammar exercises ever transfer to children's own writing. However, skills–based instruction that

1   Monroe, B. W., & Troia, G. A. (2006). Teaching writing strategies to middle school students with disabilities. *Journal of Educational Research, 100, 1,* 21–32.
2   Nicolini, M. B. (2006). Making thinking visible: Writing in the centre. *The Clearinghouse, 80, 2,* 66–69.

teaches children how to plan and compose in writing has proved to be of great benefit to those children who lack good writing skills.[3] Just as some children make optimum progress in reading if more time is spent in direct teaching of reading skills, the same principle applies in writing.

Guided writing with strategy training

Guided writing involves demonstration by the teacher or tutor of different forms of writing and how to produce them (for example, a short story, a sports report, a letter to a friend, a formal letter or a factual essay) followed by guided and independent application of the same techniques by the child. Using a whiteboard or large sheet of paper, the teacher or tutor might begin by demonstrating how to generate ideas for a given topic, how to create an opening paragraph, and how to develop the remaining ideas in logical sequence. The teacher/tutor uses 'thinking aloud' to reveal the way he or she plans and completes the task. Later, the child takes a turn to present his or her own material and receives constructive feedback from the teacher/ tutor. Children with writing difficulties need to be given a framework they can use whenever they write. They need guidance in how to begin, how to continue and how to complete the writing task.

An example of a task-approach strategy for writing uses the simple mnemonic LESSER ('LESSER helps me write MORE'). The strategy helps some children compose by providing a clear plan of action to follow.

L = List your ideas.

E = Examine your list.

S = Select your starting point.

S = Sentence one tells us about this first idea.

E = Expand on this first idea with another sentence.

R = Read what you have written. Revise if necessary. Repeat for the next paragraph.

Fountas and Pinnell[4] recommend providing writers with guidelines or checklists to help them evaluate and revise their own written work. For example, the checklist might ask:

---

3   Graham, S., & Harris, K. R. (2005). *Writing better: Effective strategies for teaching students with learning difficulties*. Baltimore: Brookes.

4   Fountas, I. C., & Pinnell, G. S. (2001). *Guiding readers and writers in Grades 3–6*. Portsmouth, NH: Heinemann.

- Did you begin with an interesting sentence?
- Are your ideas easy to understand?
- Are your ideas presented in the best sequence?
- Did you give examples to help a reader understand your points?
- Is your writing interesting?
- Have you used paragraphs?
- Have you checked spelling and punctuation?

Using a framework: cues and prompts

A teacher or tutor's role is often to stimulate the child's thinking so that writing can begin. The teacher/tutor may prepare a card with the following (or similar) prompts:

> Who? Did what? Where? When? Why? What happened? What next?

The questions (prompts) are applied to the story or topic about which the child will write. The teacher/tutor and child together jot down some brief responses to the questions. They then discuss the best sequence for presenting these ideas. First they decide upon an appropriate starting point for the story. The numeral '1' is written against that idea. How will the story develop? The child determines the order in which the other ideas will be used, and a number is written against each one. Some of the ideas may not be used at all and can be erased. The brief notes can then be elaborated into sentences, and the sentences gradually extended into paragraphs. As writing progresses, other questions may be introduced to encourage the child to become more descriptive within the writing. The additional prompts need to be tailored to match the particular theme, topic or type of writing involved. For example:

> - What does it look like (size, colour, shape)?
> - How fast would it travel?
> - What does it sound like?

By preparing the list of ideas and then discussing the best order in which to write them, the child has tackled two of the most difficult problems to be faced when composing, namely planning and sequencing. When the writing is complete, the teacher/tutor and child together edit the first draft for clarity, meaning, sequence, spelling and punctuation – with the child taking the lead if possible. The child then revises the material and produces a 'final draft' by re-writing or word processing.

Getting started is often the main obstacle faced by children who find writing difficult. One simple way of helping them complete a small story is by giving them the framework first, with some sentence beginnings to be completed using their own ideas. Children with very limited writing ability find it very much easier to complete a piece of writing when the demands of the task are reduced in this way. For example:

Anne and Sharon are good friends.
They often go together to the _____
Last time they went there they _____
Later, on the way home, they _____
They were lucky because _____
In the end _____

Temporary supports such as prompts, questions and sentence beginnings are useful for children who have difficulty at the planning stage of writing; but they must not become too dependent upon such starting points. After a suitable period of time, cues and prompts should be gradually withdrawn.

Word processors

The opportunity to use a word processor seems to be of great benefit to children who don't usually write very much and to those with the most severe spelling problems. In particular, students with learning difficulties gain confidence in creating, editing and 'publishing' their own material using a medium that holds their attention fully, puts them in control, and provides some corrective feedback.[5] When using word processors for writing, children tend to work harder and produce longer essays of better quality.

---

5   Hetzroni, O. E., & Shrieber, B. (2004). Word processing as an assistive technology tool for enhancing academic outcomes of students with writing disabilities in the general classroom. *Journal of Learning Disabilities 37*, 2, 143–54.

In a tutorial situation, the use of a computer allows the tutor to observe the writing process more directly and thus gain better insights into the child's existing skills for composing, editing and proofreading. Support can then be given to the child in any skills that are weak.

RESOURCES | **www.acer.edu.au/westwood**

Useful books on improving writing:

Graham, S., & Harris, K. R. (2005). *Writing better: Effective strategies for teaching students with learning difficulties.* Baltimore: Brookes.
Tompkins, G. E., & Blanchfield, C. L. (2005). *50 Ways to develop strategic writers.* Upper Saddle River, NJ: Pearson-Merrill-Prentice Hall.

Online information at:

DfES (Department of Education and Skills). (2005). *Raising standards in writing* available at:
http://www.standards.dfes.gov.uk/primary/publications/literacy/1160811/

Raising boys' achievements in writing available at:
http://www.standards.dfes.gov.uk/primary/publications/literacy/1094843/pns_ukla_boys094304report.pdf

General information:

http://teacher.scholastic.com/professional/teachwriting/
http://www.ldonline.org/article/6215
http://www.ncte.org/about/over/positions/category/write/118876.htm

---

Spelling

Difficulty with spelling is a frequent accompaniment to problems in reading and writing; but it is also true that a few individuals with very poor spelling are actually good readers and can write well. The problem is partly due to the fact that it is impossible to spell every single word in the English language by a simple translation from sound to letter. While almost 80 per cent of words do have reasonably predictable spelling (particularly if the writer makes efficient use of common letter groups such as –ough, –ight, –au–, –ea–, –ie–, –nk, –tion, etc), the remaining 20 per cent have letter sequences that can't easily be predicted by 'sounding out' the word. Many of these irregular words have been imported into English from other languages, while others may reflect errors made centuries ago by scribes and early print-setters.

But there are other reasons too for children's difficulties in spelling. One common reason is that too little attention has been devoted to direct teaching of spelling in primary schools in recent years. While it is true that a few children do develop spelling ability incidentally from their reading experiences and from daily writing, the majority do not. Most children need guidance to develop an understanding of the ways in which words are constructed. Teachers and tutors must play an active role in stimulating children's interest in words.[6] They also need to be taught effective strategies for learning to spell an unfamiliar word, and how to check and self-correct their own spelling. Children will not necessarily achieve accurate spelling if they are left to discover spelling principles for themselves.

The current view is that a systematic approach to spelling instruction is essential and leads to measurable improvement in children's spelling ability. By this stage in the book, it will not surprise you to know that children become better spellers as a result of direct instruction that applies the principles of modelling, imitation, feedback and practice to teach effective spelling skills and strategies.

Areas of difficulty

In attempting to work out what makes spelling difficult for a particular child, it is important to recognise that several different abilities contribute to accurate spelling. Proficiency in spelling usually requires that the following abilities be well coordinated.

- **Visual imagery:** being able to remember a word from its visual pattern or from groups of letters within it, and recognising when a spelling looks incorrect.
- **Auditory skill:** being able to identify the separate sounds that occur within a word, and then being able to represent these sounds with letters or groups of letters.

6   Sipe, L. R. (2001). Invention, convention and intervention: Invented spelling and the teacher's role. *Reading Teacher, 53, 3*, 264–273.

▶ **Kinaesthetic imagery:** being able to write or type common words automatically without thought. These words seem to be stored in memory as a movement of hand and fingers. Nichols[7] has suggested that, 'Spelling is remembered best in your hand. It is the memory of your fingers moving the pencil to make a word that makes for accurate spelling.'

▶ **Articulation skill:** being able to pronounce the word clearly and accurately in speech. Correct pronunciation of a word is a positive influence on correct spelling of that word. Some errors that children produce are the result of not saying the word correctly. Check clarity of pronunciation.

Some children with spelling difficulty rely much more heavily on one type of ability than on another, and they may need to be taught to use other skills to help construct words more accurately and to check their own spelling. Dyslexic students, for example, are often found to be particularly weak in applying auditory skills to correctly identify sounds within words. For this reason, they rely too much on inaccurate visual memory alone, resulting in the unusual spelling errors said to be typical of dyslexia. Training them to analyse words more carefully and apply basic phonic knowledge appears to have a positive effect on their spelling accuracy.

Inspection of the writing produced by children with difficulties can reveal a great deal about their current skills and specific needs in spelling. One of the most common problems with children who are not dyslexic is the tendency to be over-dependent on phonic knowledge and therefore to write all irregular words as if they are phonetically regular (for example, *sed* = said; *becos* = because; *stayshun* = station; *thay* = they). The children producing these errors seem to lack necessary strategies for carefully checking the visual appearance of a word, and often fail to identify errors even when encouraged to proofread their material. Some methods for overcoming this weakness are discussed below.

Teaching approaches

The starting point for any attempt to improve children's spelling must be to arouse their interest in words and foster a more positive attitude towards spelling. This requires that teachers and tutors themselves display infectious enthusiasm for all forms of word study.

---

7   Nichols, R. (1985). *Helping your child spell.* Earley: University of Reading.

INVESTIGATIVE APPROACH

Poulter[8] describes an approach to spelling in which children study groups of words, identify letter-groups shared by different words, deduce any rules that may be operating in particular word families, and use this information to spell unfamiliar words. Poulter explains the principle in these terms:

> An investigative and problem-solving approach helps pupils become more confident about unknown words. They realise that the English language has some rules that are useful and many that are broken. Perhaps more importantly, children become interested in words, more enthusiastic about the vocabulary they encounter in all areas of life, and more prepared to have a go at spelling them.

Massengill[9] describes a similar approach called 'Interactive Word Study', a method for helping children examine, compare, discriminate and make judgments about letter sequences needed to represent units of sound and meaning. This researcher also remarked that having been exposed to the word study approach, children reported gains in confidence in their own ability to spell difficult words.

Many teachers now use an activity called *Word Sorts*. Children are provided with cards containing a set of words to be studied and compared. The words might be: *sock, black, truck, lock, rack, trick, track, block, lick, sack, stick, flock, flick, suck, luck.* Teachers ask the students, 'What is the same about these words?' The response might be that the words all end with /ck/. The words might now be categorised in other ways by sorting the cards into groups (for example, words ending in /ock/; words ending in /ack/). At a more advanced level, Word Sorts could involve words that are grouped according to the meaning–spelling connection, for example, *played, playfully, replay, player, playground, horseplay.*

STRATEGY TRAINING

In order to avoid inefficient rote memorisation method, which is often adopted by weaker spellers, it is important to teach them effective ways of approaching an unfamiliar word. There can be no doubt that improvement

8   Poulter, M. (2002). Focus on spelling. *Literacy Today, 32*, 10–11.

9   Massengill, D. (2006). Mission accomplished, it's learnable now: Voices of mature challenged spellers using a word study approach. *Journal of Adolescent and Adult Literacy, 49*, 5, 420–431.

in spelling can be achieved when students are taught more about *how to learn words* and *how to check* the spelling of the words they have attempted. Competent spellers possess a range of effective spelling strategies and can apply them appropriately as needed. Let us look now at some useful spelling strategies.

> *Think – Try – Check*

A typical self-help spelling strategy to teach a child involves applying the following steps:

▶ saying the word
▶ repeating the word slowly
▶ counting the syllables
▶ writing the syllables in sequence, matching letters and letter groups to sounds
▶ checking the result carefully while again saying the word slowly
▶ checking the visual appearance of the word
▶ repeating the process if necessary until satisfied
▶ checking with other sources if still not satisfied (dictionary, spell-checker, another student or adult).

> *Look–Say–Cover–Write–Check (LSCWC)*

This strategy encourages accurate visual imagery. It is very effective for learning words that contain irregular letter-to-sound correspondences (for example, *choir*). Ask children to:

▶ Look at the word carefully.
▶ Say the word clearly. Try to remember every detail.
▶ Cover the word so that it cannot be seen.
▶ Write the word from memory, pronouncing it quietly as you write.
▶ Check your version of the word with the original. If it is not correct, go back through the steps again until you can produce the word accurately.
▶ For some children, finger tracing over the word may help them to remember the letter sequence.
▶ Check for recall several days later.

The look-say-cover-write-check approach is far better than any rote learning procedure for learning to spell. It gives the child an independent system that can be applied to the study of any irregular words set for homework or to corrections from free writing. The strategy, although regarded as a visual learning method, is almost certainly effective because children are identifying *groups of letters* that represent *pronounceable parts* of words. From the earlier chapter on reading skills, we know that this is precisely the type of information that is also essential for swift and efficient word recognition. Kelly[10] strongly advocates teaching children useful strategies to help them study key features of the target word at the stage when they are 'looking and saying' in the sequence above.

> Sound spelling

This phonic strategy is simply building on a child's natural tendency to invent the spelling of a word based on the syllables and sounds he or she can hear within the word. The child is encouraged to analyse the unfamiliar word into units of sound, and then represent these sounds by groups of letters. Again, the word must be checked visually after it has been written.

> Spelling by analogy

This strategy encourages children to use a spelling they already know to help with the spelling of an unfamiliar word that sounds similar. For example, knowing how to spell 'east' helps with the spelling of new words such as 'least', 'yeast' or 'easterly'. The effective use of *word families* (see Chapter 7) is one way of helping children notice and remember common elements contained within and across words.

> Simultaneous Oral Spelling (SOS)

This strategy is particularly useful for older students (upper primary, secondary and adult) because it uses alphabet names for letters, not sounds. The approach involves six steps:

▶ The child selects the word they wish to learn. They ask the teacher/tutor to pronounce it clearly.

▶ The child pronounces the word clearly while looking carefully at the word.

---

10 Kelly, G. (2006). A check on Look, Cover, Write, Check. *Bulletin: Learning Difficulties Australia*. *38, 1*, 6–7.

- The child says each syllable in the word (or break a single-syllable word into onset and rime).
- The child names all the letters in the word twice.
- The child writes the word, naming each letter as they write it.
- The child checks the word.

> *Repeated writing*

The practice of having a child correct an error by writing the correct version of the word several times is believed by some teachers to be a waste of time. They consider that it can be carried out without any conscious effort on the part of the learner, and so words practised in this way are not remembered later. However, repeated writing of a target word can be very helpful indeed if (i) the learner has every intention of trying to remedy an error; and (ii) if he or she is attending fully to the task. It is one way in which kinaesthetic images of words can be more firmly established. Only a few words (*no more than three*) should be practised in any one session.

> *Old Way—New Way*

Old Way–New Way[11] uses the child's error as the starting point for change. A memory of the old (incorrect) way of spelling of the word is used to remind the child of the new (correct) way of spelling the word. The following steps are used.

- The child writes the word in the usual (incorrect) form.
- The teacher/tutor and child agree to call this the 'old way' of spelling that word.
- The teacher/tutor shows the child a 'new way' (correct way) of spelling the word.
- The teacher/tutor draws attention to the similarities and differences between the old and the new forms.
- The child writes word again in the old way.
- The child writes word in the new way, and *states clearly the differences*.
- The teacher/tutor and child repeat five such writings of old way, new way and statement of differences.

---

11 Lyndon, H. (1989). 'I did it my way': an introduction to Old Way–New Way. *Australasian Journal of Special Education, 13*, 32–7.

- The child writes the word the new way six times, using different colour pens or in different styles.
- Older children may be asked to write six different sentences using the word in its 'new' form.
- Revise the word or words after one week and then again after two weeks.
- If necessary, repeat this procedure at intervals until the new response is firmly established.

RESOURCES | www.acer.edu.au/westwood

Useful books on teaching spelling include:

Nunes, T., & Bryant, P. (2006). *Improving literacy by teaching morphemes.* London: Routledge.
O'Sullivan, O., & Thomas, A. (2007). *Understanding spelling.* London: Routledge.

Information on 'word study' is available online at:

http://www.geocities.com/Athens/Troy/7175/word2.htm
http://www.phon.ucl.ac.uk/home/dick/tta/spelling/teaching.htm

Useful word lists covering general writing needs and specific spelling vocabulary for different subjects within the school curriculum can be located online at:

http://www.phon.ucl.ac.uk/home/dick/tta/spelling/ks3list.htm

For children with learning difficulties, practical advice is offered at:

http://www.csusm.edu/Quiocho/sp.students.htm

KEY POINTS FOR PARENTS

- Children improve their writing by doing more writing and receiving positive feedback.

>>

▶ Writing can be made easier for children if they are taught effective plans of action to use as they write.

▶ Writing in the early stages can be made easier if children are provided with support.

▶ The starting point for improving spelling is to arouse children's genuine interest in words.

▶ Analysing words into syllables and identifying sounds within syllables is an aid to spelling.

▶ Effective instruction does not set out to teach children how to spell every individual word they may need in their writing. Instead, they are taught strategies for learning to spell any word.

▶ Within each tutorial session, children should work on specific words misspelled in free writing lessons as well as on more general word lists or word families.

▶ When making a correction to a word, a child should *rewrite the whole word* not merely erase the incorrect letters.

▶ It is useful to have a range of games, word puzzles and computer tasks available to reinforce the spelling of important words.

▶ Don't spend time asking children to spell words aloud without writing them down. It is always necessary to write and check.

ten
Difficulties with basic mathematics

Many children – with and without disabilities or learning difficulties – find mathematics a difficult subject. More adults are prepared to admit 'I was never any good at maths' than would ever admit to having had problems with reading. Somehow, being poor at mathematics carries no stigma at all in society. Perhaps the very nature of the subject matter, and the way in which understanding of higher-level concepts and processes requires that all simpler levels have been thoroughly mastered, makes mathematics a very challenging subject for any learner.

To some extent, the way in which mathematics is supposed to be taught in schools today has added to the problem. As a result of reforms in mathematics education that started in the late 1980s, schools are now expected to implement an 'investigative' or 'problem-based' approach to mathematics learning.[1] Rather than using methods that focus mainly on developing children's arithmetic skills, teachers are encouraged, even in primary school, to create learning situations that provide opportunities to *discover* mathematical relationships by investigating and solving problems. It is believed that children will develop facility in applying number skills through such activities, rather than spending time doing pages and pages of routine arithmetic calculations. However, critics now suggest that a problem-based approach makes unreasonable assumptions concerning children's ability to discover *and remember* mathematical relationships for themselves. The evidence seems to indicate that not all children make good progress under an activity approach, particularly in the beginning stages of learning something new; some students clearly make much better

---

1   National Council of Teachers of Mathematics (US). (2005). *Overview: Principles for school mathematics.* Online at: http://standards.nctm.org/document/chapter2/index.htm

progress in mathematics when they are directly taught.[2] In particular, there is major concern over the reduced attention now given to developing children's automaticity in essential computational skills.

Although the findings are to some extent contrary to the direction taken by the reform movement, the research on teacher effectiveness in the area of mathematics supports the use of a structured approach within a carefully sequenced program. The most effective teachers of mathematics appear to provide systematic instruction in such a way that children not only master arithmetic skills and problem-solving strategies, but also develop a genuine understanding of the subject matter.

Effective teaching of mathematics certainly places emphasis upon constructing meaning rather than memorisation and rote learning; but this is not achieved successfully simply through the medium of unstructured activities. Effective lessons are typically clear, accurate and rich in examples of a particular concept, process or strategy. The teacher/tutor takes an active role in stimulating students' thinking, imparting relevant information, and teaching specific skills. Lessons are conducted at a reasonably fast pace and incorporate a high degree of student participation and practice. Every effort is made to help students transfer and generalise ideas and processes taught in school to real-life problems and situations. The emerging perspective is that effective teaching and learning in mathematics requires not only student-centred investigative activities but also a good measure of teacher-directed explicit instruction.[3] Effective mathematics teaching is all about striking the right balance between teaching number facts and calculation procedures on the one hand and developing a good conceptual understanding and generalisation on the other.[4]

Whatever teaching approach is used in the classroom, it is essential to help a child develop functional arithmetic skills and effective problem-solving strategies. Functional knowledge in arithmetic involves two major components: mastery of basic number facts that can be automatically retrieved from memory (for example, $7 + 3$; 10×9; $12 \div 3$; $11 - 5$, etc.)

---

2   Farkota, R. (2005). Basic math problems: The brutal reality! *Learning Difficulties Australia Bulletin 37, 3,* 10–11.

3   Hay, I., Elias, G., & Booker, G. (2005). Students with learning difficulties in relation to literacy and numeracy. *Schooling Issues Digest 2005/1.* Canberra: Department of Education, Science and Training. Online at: http://dest.gov.au/schools/publications/digest.

4   Nelson, B., & Sassi, A. (2007). What math teachers need most. *Education Digest, 72, 6,* 54–56.

and a body of knowledge about computational procedures for subtraction, addition, multiplication and division. On top of these competencies, children also need problem-solving strategies to apply when faced with any mathematical problem or situation.

In years gone by, with a purely textbook approach, too little attention was given to ensuring that students were able to transfer and *apply* arithmetic skills and mathematical concepts to a wide variety of everyday contexts. Boaler[5] states that, 'In real-world situations these students were disabled in two ways. Not only were they unable to use the math they had learned because they could not adapt it to fit unfamiliar situations, but they could not see the relevance of this acquired math knowledge from school for situations outside the classroom' (p. 30). It is vital that teachers, tutors and parents recognise that skill in arithmetic is a necessary *but insufficient* component of competence in functional mathematics. Children do require extensive experience in applying number skills and concepts for many different and meaningful purposes. But I make no apology in this chapter for stressing the careful teaching of arithmetic skills. The National Council of Teachers of Mathematics (US) (2000) affirms that all students should develop fluency in operations with numbers, using swift mental computation and paper-and-pencil calculations.[6]

Areas of difficulty

As stated in the opening paragraph, a significant number of children display a poor attitude towards mathematics and have no confidence in their own ability to improve. Some exhibit definite anxiety or panic in situations where they are expected to demonstrate competence in applying mathematical skills. A very small number of these students may have a specific learning disability related to mathematics (*dyscalculia*) but most have simply encountered difficulties for a variety of different reasons and have developed learned helplessness.

Some of the factors associated with learning difficulties in mathematics include:

---

5   Boaler, J. (1999). Mathematics for the moment, or the millennium? *Education Week, 18, 29*, 30–31.

6   National Council of Teachers of Mathematics (US). (2000). *Principles and standards for school mathematics*. Reston, VA: NCTM.

- insufficient or inappropriate instruction
- curriculum content covered too rapidly, outstripping the child's ability to keep up
- too much time devoted to discovery learning – a child may fail to learn or remember anything from them
- too little time spent developing automaticity with tables and number facts leading later to slowness and inaccuracy in calculations
- the teacher's/tutor's level of language when explaining mathematical relationships or posing questions may be above the child's level of comprehension
- abstract symbols are introduced too early, in the absence of real-life examples
- child has difficulty understanding place-value (for example, that in the number 111 the first numeral on the left represents 100 while the final numeral represents 1 unit)
- reading difficulties associated with the textbook or problem-sheet.
- difficulty comprehending the exact meaning of specific mathematical terms
- in problem solving, not really understanding what is being asked
- uncertainty about which process or processes (**+**, **×** or **÷**) to use to obtain an answer
- lack of effective strategies for approaching mathematical tasks
- inability to transfer mathematical skills taught in school to the real world.

Many children with learning difficulties have problems learning and recalling basic number facts and multiplication tables. They may waste much time counting on fingers or working out simple facts with a pocket calculator. Number facts need to be recalled with a high degree of speed and automaticity so that they do not take up time and mental effort when solving larger problems. Knowing number facts is partly a matter of learning them through repetition, and partly a matter of grasping a rule (for example, that zero added to any number doesn't change it: $3 + 0 = 3$, $13 + 0 = 13$; or if $7 + 3 = 10$ then $7 + 4$ must be 'one more than ten', etc.). Such understanding is now referred to as having 'good number sense'.[7] Regular practice will help develop the necessary automaticity. Some of this practice can be achieved through traditional speed-and-accuracy worksheets or by using number activities presented on the computer screen.

---

7 Howell, S. & Kemp, C. (2006). An international perspective of early number sense. *Australian Journal of Learning Disabilities, 11, 4*, 197–207.

Teaching approaches

A diagnostic approach

The first step in helping a child with difficulties in basic mathematics should be to find out what he or she can already do in this area of the curriculum. It is also essential to locate any specific gaps in knowledge which may exist, and to determine what he or she needs to be taught next.

Using a sheet of appropriately graded arithmetic problems as a focus, a discussion between teacher/tutor and child can reveal much about the child's level of confidence, flexibility in thinking, and underlying knowledge and skills. Starting with the easiest examples and working towards the more difficult, use the following questions as a guide as you attempt to discover the child's functional level. When the child fails to solve a particular arithmetic example, consider:

- *Why* did the child get this item wrong?
- Can he or she carry out the process if allowed to use counters, count on fingers, use a number line or calculator?
- Can he or she explain to me what to do to carry out this calculation or solve this problem? Ask the child to work through the example step by step, thinking aloud at each step. At what point does the child make the error? If a child explains how he or she tackles the problem, the teacher/tutor can pick up at once on the exact point of confusion and can teach from there. Too often the teacher/tutor quickly re-teaches *the whole process*, but the child still fails to recognise and overcome the precise point of difficulty.

To explore the child's ability to solve word problems, a teacher/tutor should probe for understanding in the following areas. Can the child:

- understand what is called for in the problem
- identify relevant information to use
- select correct arithmetic process
- estimate an approximate answer
- calculate the answer accurately
- check the final answer, and self-correct if necessary?

Teaching mechanical arithmetic skills

The term 'mechanical arithmetic' simply means the process of setting down numbers in a particular horizontal or vertical format and carrying out the necessary steps to add, subtract, multiply or divide those numbers. Children often refer to this as 'doing sums' (although technically the word 'sum' should really only be applied to addition examples).

Each of the four processes for addition, subtraction, multiplication or division has its own set of steps to follow in order to obtain the correct answer. It is, of course, traditional to teach children verbal cues to use when carrying out the steps in a particular calculation. For example, in this subtraction item the child would be taught to verbalise the steps in some way similar to the wording below. You can probably still recall the words you were taught to use when you were at school.

H T U	The child says: 'Start with the units. I can't take 9 from 2 so I must borrow a ten and write it next to the 2 to make 12. I cross out the 8 tens and write 7 tens.
6 7̸8̸ 1̸2	
–2 3 9	
4 4 3	Now, I can take 9 from 12 units and write 3 in the units column.
	In the tens column, 7 tens take away 3 tens leaves 4 tens. I write 4 in the tens column.
	In the hundreds column, 6 hundreds take away 2 hundreds leaves 4 hundreds. I write 4 in the hundreds column.
	My answer is 443.
	I will check that: 443 + 239 = 682. Correct!'

Teachers in different schools may teach slightly different verbal cues. Parents who attempt to help a child with mechanical arithmetic must find out from the teacher the precise verbal cues that are used in teaching the four processes in that school so that exactly the same words and directions can be used at home to avoid confusion. Verbal cueing is only required during the time a child is first mastering a new process. Once it is mastered, the procedure becomes automatic.

Learning arithmetic in this way has fallen somewhat into disrepute in recent years. Some experts feel that it represents nothing more than rote learning. They fear that children may 'learn the tricks' but not really understand the concept behind processes such as long division or multiplying fractions. However, without verbal cues for working through a calculation step by step, children with learning difficulties are likely to remain totally confused and frustrated.

Parents often wonder what the role of the pocket calculator is in learning basic maths. The consensus of opinion on this issue is that basic computational skills are best taught initially without the use of calculator because children need to learn and understand the processes. Once they become proficient in mental and paper-and-pencil work, calculators can be used for checking answers and for solving more complex problems.[8]

The Old Way–New Way method, described already in Chapter 9, can also help children remedy specific errors in carrying out calculations.[9] It is believed that this method helps a learner remember a correct procedure. The steps involved are:

▶ When a child makes an error in calculation the tutor says, 'We will call this the *Old Way* of doing it'. 'I will show you the *New Way*'.

▶ Tutor demonstrates the correct way of calculating and calls it the 'New Way'.

▶ Child and tutor together compare and discuss the differences between Old and New.

▶ Child performs the *Old Way* again, then *New Way* again, and clearly points out and describes the differences.

▶ Child then repeats five more *Old Way/New Way* cycles, each time comparing and contrasting the two models.

It is important to correct children's errors as soon as they occur. If they practise incorrect procedures these become firmly established and it is difficult later to remedy the weakness.

---

8   Greer, S. (2006). A study of the effect of calculator use on computational skills of high school students. In L. P. McCoy (Ed.) *Studies in teaching 2006: Research digest* (pp. 61–66). Winston-Salem, NC: Wake Forest University.

9   Dole, S. (2003). Applying psychological theory to helping students overcome learned difficulties in mathematics: an alternative approach to intervention. *School Psychology International, 24, 1,* 95–114.

Developing problem-solving strategies

Children with learning difficulties usually display learned helplessness and confusion when faced with mathematical problems in word form. They may, for example, have difficulty reading the problem and comprehending the exact meaning of specific terms. They do not know how or where to begin, or what process to use. Their most obvious weakness is a lack of any effective plan of action for approaching a mathematical task. Children with these difficulties need to be taught a range of effective problem-solving and task-approach strategies. The aim is to teach them how to process information in a word problem without a feeling of panic or hopelessness. They need to be able to sift information sensibly and impose some degree of structure for solving the problem.

It is generally accepted that there are recognisable and teachable steps involved in solving mathematical problems. These steps can be summarised as:

▶ interpretation of the problem
▶ identification of processes and steps needed
▶ translation of the information into an appropriate calculation
▶ accurate completion of the calculation
▶ checking the result.

The child needs to approach the word problem with the help of some self-directing questions. For example:

▶ **Identify the problem:** 'What do I need to work out in this problem?'
▶ **Select a strategy:** 'How will I try to do this?'
▶ **Visualise the problem:** 'Can I picture this problem in my mind?'
▶ **Self-monitoring:** 'Is this working out OK?'
▶ **Evaluation:** 'How will I check if my solution is correct?'
▶ **Self-checking; self-correction:** 'I need to correct this error and then try again' … 'This looks better'.

When teaching a problem-solving strategy the teacher/tutor needs to:

▶ model and demonstrate use of the strategy for solving routine and non-routine problems
▶ 'think aloud' as various aspects of the problem are analysed

▶ discuss possible procedures for calculating a result
▶ reflect upon the effectiveness of the procedure and the result obtained.

A problem-solving strategy might, for example, use a particular mnemonic to aid recall of the procedure. For example, in the mnemonic 'RAVE CCC' the word RAVE can be used to identify the first four possible steps to take:

R = Read the problem carefully.
A = Attend to words that may suggest the process to use (for example, *share, altogether, less than*).
V = Visualise the problem, and perhaps make a sketch or diagram.
E = Estimate the possible answer.

Then the letters CCC suggest what to do next:

C = Choose the numbers to use.
C = Calculate the answer.
C = Check the answer against your estimate.

Once children have been taught a particular strategy they need an opportunity to apply the strategy themselves under guidance and with feedback. Finally, they must be able to use the strategy independently and to generalise its use to other problems. The sequence for teaching problem solving to students with learning difficulties therefore follows a sequence beginning with direct teaching, followed by guided practice, and ending with student-centred control and independent use.

Additional teaching points to consider when improving the problem-solving abilities of students with learning difficulties include:

▶ pre-teaching any difficult vocabulary associated with a specific word problem so that comprehension is enhanced
▶ providing cues (such as directional arrows) to indicate where to begin calculations and in which direction to proceed
▶ linking problems to the students' own life experiences
▶ giving children experience in setting their own problems for others to solve
▶ stressing self-checking and praising self-correction.

It is clear that for students with learning difficulties it is necessary to provide many more examples than usual to establish and strengthen the application of a particular strategy. Since there is evidence that children can be helped to become more proficient at solving problems, teachers of children with learning difficulties need to devote more time to this important area of schoolwork.

RESOURCES | **www.acer.edu.au/westwood**

Useful books on basic mathematics include:

Booker, G., Bond, D., Sparrow, L. & Swan, P. (2004). *Teaching primary mathematics* (3rd ed.). Melbourne: Pearson-Longman.
Chinn, S. (2004). *The trouble with maths: a practical guide to helping learners with numeracy difficulties*, London: RoutledgeFalmer.
Westwood, P. (2000). *Numeracy and learning difficulties*. Melbourne: Australian Council *for* Educational Research.

Online resources include:

Dowker, A. (2004) *What works for children with mathematical difficulties?* Research Report RR554, London: DfES, at: http://www.dfes.gov.uk/research/data/uploadfiles/RR554.pdf_http://www.ldonline.org/indepth/math
http://www.edfac.melbourne.edu/eldi/selage/documents/MLDT-Diagnoselearndif.pdf
http://www.ncld.org/index.php?option=content&task=view&id=463
http://www.qca.org.uk/qca_1855.aspx

KEY POINTS FOR PARENTS

▶ Mathematics is thought by many children to be a tough subject to learn.
▶ In order to solve mathematical problems quickly and easily, children need to have basic number skills firmly established.
▶ Children also need to be taught effective strategies for approaching word problems in an efficient and confident manner.
▶ Direct teaching, followed by abundant successful practice, is needed to make mathematics accessible for all children.

▶ Direct teaching needs to be combined with an investigative approach to ensure that children not only become proficient in arithmetic but can also use those skills for solving problems and for everyday purposes.

Appendix A

Basic sight vocabulary

THE FIRST 110 MOST COMMONLY OCCURRING WORDS, IN DESCENDING ORDER OF FREQUENCY

This list can be used for teaching or assessment purposes. For teaching, the list can provide appropriate words to include in word recognition games and flashcard work. For assessment, the list can be used as a simple test to reveal which of the words are not yet known by the child and, therefore, need further practice.

the	I	at	from	been
of	for	have	she	their
and	that	are	which	has
a	you	not	or	would
in	he	this	we	there
to	be	but	an	what
it	with	had	were	will
is	on	they	as	all
was	by	his	do	if

can	its	only	well	many
her	then	just	should	years
said	two	more	like	those
who	out	these	than	go
one	time	also	how	being
so	my	people	get	because
up	about	know	way	down
them	did	any	our	three
some	your	first	made	good
when	now	see	got	back
could	me	very	after	make
him	no	new	think	such
into	other	may	between	over

Appendix B

Basic letter knowledge

Can the child recognise and name these letters?
Can the child tell you the common *sound* represented by each letter?

SINGLE LETTERS

A ɑ a	B b	C c
D d	E e	F f
G G g g	H h	I i
J j	K k	L l
M m	N n	O o
P p	Q q	R r
S s	T t	U u
V v	W w	X x x
Y y	Z z	

COMMON INITIAL CONSONANT DIGRAPHS

sh	th	ch
wh	qu	ph

COMMON CONSONANT BLENDS

st	sp	sc
sk	sl	sw
sn	sm	br
bl	cr	dr
pr	tr	gr
fr	pl	cl
fl	gl	tw

COMMON THREE-LETTER BLENDS

str	spl	thr
scr	shr	spr
squ		

Appendix C

Phonic units

COMMON RIME UNITS FOR BUILDING SIMPLE ONE-SYLLABLE WORD FAMILIES

These units can provide a child with simple word-building experience. Once a child has moved beyond single-letter, decoding it is helpful to maintain his or her confidence and ability by using rime units and adding one or two letters at the front for reading and simple spelling practice. The units can be used within card games, word family exercises, or for informal assessment.

–an	–ap	–at	–ad	–ag
–am	–ed	–eg	–en	–et
–ib	–id	–in	–it	–ip
–ob	–od	–og	–op	–ot
–ub	–ug	–um	–un	–up
–ut	–ack	–ail	–ain	–ake
–ale	–ame	–and	–amp	–ank
–ash	–ate	–ask	–ay	–eat
–eck	–ell	–est	–esh	–imp

–ice	–ick	–ide	–ill	–ine
–ing	–ink	–ight	–ock	–oke
–ope	–uck	–ump	–unk	–ung

OTHER USEFUL LETTER STRINGS

–ight	–ough	–ought	–aught	–dge
–ance	–ence	–ange	–ose	–are
–tion	–ttle	–ddle	–tter	–bble
–cket	–ckle	–stle	–able	–ture
–ssion	–ible	–ious	–ent	–tial
–cial	–erve	–ieve	–tor	–tain

Quiz answers

1   **Learning problems in children are always due to a learning disability.**
    The statement is definitely FALSE. Chapter 2 presents a variety of reasons to account for learning difficulty; a learning disability is only one possible cause out of many.

2   **Children are naturally lazy when it comes to reading school textbooks.**
    Again, this is FALSE. Children are not 'naturally' lazy about anything. It is true that they may find school textbooks less interesting and more difficult to understand, compared to comics and magazines. They may therefore be reluctant to devote time to school books; but this is not laziness. Actually, it is a natural reaction to boredom and frustration.

3   **All children with reading problems should be referred to as 'dyslexic'.**
    Again the statement is FALSE. Dyslexia (a specific learning disability) is the cause of reading failure in only about 2 per cent of the school population. Given that studies have shown some 16 per cent of school children have difficulties with reading and spelling or mathematics, obviously not all of them are dyslexic. Their difficulties are due to influences discussed in Chapter 2.

4   **Which of the following are true?**
    It is not easy to give a definitive 'yes' or 'no' to some of the following suggestions. Please read the additional comments below each item.

    To help my child overcome learning difficulties in reading, spelling or mathematics I should:
    ☑ **provide support and encouragement at home**
        This is an essential component in helping your child in a positive way. If done skilfully, this is unlikely to cause him or her to rebel against you or to resent your intrusion.

☒ put pressure on my child to make him or her work harder

This is one of the surest ways of making a situation worse. The child is already 'under pressure' at school. You will probably ruin your chances of establishing a good working relationship with your child if you adopt this approach.

☒ extend homework time every evening until progress is made

Just how bad do you want this child to feel? Do not make homework into a fraught and tense situation; and don't continue forcing study beyond the child's limits of attention and concentration. The child has already had a long day at school, and is probably frustrated by problems and teachers' comments.

☒ give my child more difficult books or maths problems as a challenge

For some reason, many parents seem to think that reading skills will develop if children are forced to read books at a higher level of difficulty, or that maths skills will improved by setting harder problems. In both cases, it is extremely frustrating and de-motivating for the child to struggle with material that is way above his or her current ability.

☒ indicate to the child how worried you are by his difficulties

Even though you are worried, it doesn't help to signal your deep concern to the child. It may make him or her feel even worse, and depressed. In a few cases, children begin to feel powerful (in a negative way) because they can cause such a level of concern in parents. They can begin to use this power in a manipulative way.

☑ show interest in his or her school work

Again, this is a positive thing to do. But don't be surprised if your child is reluctant to share much with you. Many children are like that. Encourage sharing ... but don't push it.

☐ hire a private tutor for after-school coaching

This is for you to decide. Remember that to have any real value, such coaching needs to be several times a week, not just once. You are also adding significantly to the length of the child's school day, which may breed resentment. In addition, you may be creating a situation where you must commit yourself daily to picking the child up from school and from the tutor, and this becomes an ongoing burden. Finally, do understand that not every tutor is effective, some are not trained in remedial teaching strategies, and you may be wasting your time and money.

☐ **request that the school has your child assessed by a psychologist**
In some schools it is necessary to have children formally assessed by an educational psychologist in order to qualify for additional support and remedial tutoring. You have the right to make such a request; but based on their professional judgment and experience, school staff may suggest to you that this is unnecessary. Remember that referring your child to a psychologist may make the child feel very 'different' from classmates. It can be the beginning of a feeling that 'There is something wrong with me. Am I crazy?'

☐ **take your child to a psychologist yourself**
Again, that is your decision; but the point about making the child feel weird and different (see above) applies here too. To a child, seeing a psychologist seems rather like going to see a doctor because 'something is wrong with me'. Experience over many years in education has indicated to me that the report a parent typically gets from a psychologist simply confirms what they already know – that the child is having difficulties in certain school subjects. This will be accompanied by test results, including an IQ score, but since psychologists are not experts in curriculum and teaching methods their advice tends to be lacking in practical aspects for what the parents or teachers should do.

☒ **take your child to your family doctor**
This is not usually necessary, unless you think your child has hearing, vision or health problems. Most GPs are not expert in learning difficulties and they are likely merely to refer your child on to a psychologist for assessment. All this creates a very unnecessary and inappropriate 'medical' and 'clinical' atmosphere surrounding your child's problem.

☒ **remove privileges, such as TV time and computer games, until progress is made**
There might be the odd occasion when loss of privileges is an appropriate response, but in general all it will do is create hostility and non-compliance in the child. Try to look for more positive ways of encouraging your child to work hard. Praise for effort is worth much more than punishments or penalties.

☐ **provide rewards each time when school reports are better**
Most parents (and teachers) find the judicious use of rewards can be motivating. Maybe a good report is one appropriate occasion.

☒ **all the above.**

Definitely not. Some of the suggestions are not helpful – and may indeed be harmful.

5 **An important concept in the psychology of learning is 'automaticity'. What does this term mean?**

The term *automaticity*, as applied in learning theory, describes the situation where an individual has become so proficient at carrying out certain processes (for example, recognising words in print, recalling number facts, handwriting, or using a keyboard) that he or she no longer needs to think about what they are doing …. the skill has become *automatic*. Automaticity is highly desirable in basic skills such as reading, spelling and calculating with numbers. The reasons are explained in Chapter 6.

6 **Another important concept is 'motivation'. What does this mean; and how does it influence learning?**

According to Ormrod (2000, p. 472)[1] 'Motivation is something that energizes, directs, and sustains behaviour; it gets students moving, points them in a particular direction, and keeps them going'. Sometimes children are motivated by their interest in a particular subject and by the satisfaction their efforts bring. At other times it is necessary to provide incentives or rewards to motivate children to do something. These two types of motivation, intrinsic and extrinsic, are discussed in Chapter 2 and Chapter 6.

7 **It is no longer necessary for children to memorise multiplication tables and other number facts because they can use a pocket calculator.**

False. Even in this age of information and communication technology, it is still important to be able to work mentally with numbers. Developing automaticity with numbers allows an individual to deal with mathematical problems and computations more quickly and easily.

8 **Learning the relationship between letters and the sounds they represent is an essential step in learning to read and spell.**

True. The importance of teaching phonic principles to children in the early stages of learning to read and spell is explained in Chapter 7 and Chapter 9. Research fully supports this view.

---

1   Ormrod, J. (2000). *Educational psychology* (3rd ed.). Columbus: OH: Merrill.

9 **Have you ever found it difficult to learn something new? If so, how did you deal with the problem?**

The chances are that, like the rest of us, you found something that was difficult to learn at some time in your life. If you were generally confident at the time in your own ability to learn other things (psychologists call this having a positive view of your own self-efficacy), you probably persevered, and eventually conquered the new learning. Or maybe you gave up and decided that you didn't want to learn it anyway. (This applied to me when I tried to learn to water-ski, and when I attempted to learn to speak Cantonese. For me, big failures! I gave up.) Remember that children in school can't simply 'give up'. They still have to endure lessons in the difficult subject every day.

10 **Computer programs can be helpful in improving children's basic literacy and numeracy skills. Do you agree? Why?**

It is true that well designed instructional software can definitely help children apply and strengthen their basic skills. The computer provides abundant opportunities for successful practice, and therefore helps develop automaticity. Computer-assisted learning is also intrinsically motivating because the child is controlling the session, making active responses, and getting immediate feedback. The computer tends to have more patience than the average teacher/tutor.

Glossary

Activity-based methods: These represent a teaching and learning approach that involves children in acquiring new knowledge and skills through their own actions and explorations. The children may use resource materials or real-life situations to gain new understandings and apply new skills. Activity methods often involve cooperative groupwork.

Audiologist: An expert in assessing children's hearing.

Automaticity: This term describes the ability to carry out a familiar skill or recall information without conscious effort. Automaticity is acquired through frequent practice of a skill.

Computational skills: A term meaning the skills involved in calculating with numbers. The skills include steps and processes in adding, subtracting, multiplying and dividing.

Consonant blends: Many words use two or more consonants occurring together in their spelling. Examples include *dr, pl, st, str* (see also Appendix B). When pronouncing a consonant blend one can still identify the two or three separate sounds that are represented. Automatic recognition of blends is essential in efficient reading and spelling.

Contextual cues in reading: It is often possible to guess some of the words within a sentence you are reading because the meaning of the sentence makes them highly predictable. Teachers refer to this as 'using context' to supplement word recognition and decoding.

Corrective feedback: When we provide children with comments on their work we usually include correction of any significant errors they have made and suggestions for improvement.

Decoding: This term, when applied to reading, usually refers to the use of phonic knowledge to sound out an unfamiliar word. The reverse process is *encoding*, as for example when phonic knowledge is applied to spelling.

Digraphs: These are two letters that, when used together as a unit, produce only one speech sound. Examples are *ch*, *th*, *wh*. They differ from consonant blends where each letter retains something of its own separate sound.

Discovery learning: This is an activity-based method in which children find out information and develop concepts through their own efforts rather than having the information presented directly to them by the teacher. It is a method that usually motivates children very well; but it does not always lead to high-quality learning.

Dyscalculia: A specific disability in learning to deal with arithmetic and problem solving. It is not a term that should be applied lightly to all children who find mathematics difficult. To diagnose dyscalculia, the child must be of at least average intelligence and have had normal opportunities to learn. Assessment by a psychologist is necessary to identify this disability.

Dyslexia: A specific disability that seriously impairs an individual's ability to learn to read, write and spell. The individual is of at least average intelligence, has no other significant handicap, and has been exposed to normal teaching. Assessment by a psychologist is necessary to identify this disability.

Extrinsic motivation: This type of motivational influence comes from outside the individual, usually in the form of an anticipated reward or pleasant consequence for engaging in a particular activity. Extrinsic motivation often needs to be provided for children with learning difficulties because they are not self-motivated to engage in tasks that they find difficult or unpleasant.

Generalisation: In learning theory, this term refers to the way in which new learning achieved in one situation can be used later by the learner in other appropriate situations. It is difficult to ensure that children with learning problems will transfer and generalise new learning, so teaching of that skill or strategy often has to be repeated in a number of different contexts.

Intrinsic motivation: This motivational influence comes from within the learner and from the task he or she is attempting. For example, a child may willingly read a book or magazine article about a favourite pop singer because of genuine personal interest, curiosity and satisfaction. No reward or pressure is needed to get them to do this. On the other hand, to get them to read a history textbook would require extrinsic motivation, such as a promise that they can watch TV after they complete the assignment.

Learned helplessness: As a result of many experiences of failure, a child may come to believe that he or she will never manage to improve. The child becomes passive, dependent and unresponsive to normal degrees of encouragement.

Mnemonic: A simple trick or device to help one remember something.

Onset-rime: A simple but very important term used to indicate that even single-syllable words can be broken into two pronounceable parts – the beginning sound (onset), and the vowel and all that follows it (rime). Example: /sh/ – /ut/ = shut.

Phoneme: A speech sound.

Phonemic awareness: The ability to analyse spoken words into their separate sounds.

Phonics: The association between speech sounds and the letters or letter groups used to represent them in print and writing. The term *phonics* can also be used to refer to the decoding process that uses letter-to-sound relationships to read and spell unfamiliar words.

Phonological awareness: A more general term than *phonemic awareness*. Phonological awareness covers not only the ability to detect similarity and difference between speech sounds, but also rhyme, alliteration and blending.

Place value: An important concept in understanding numbers. It refers to awareness of the value of a digit by reference to its position in a large number. For example, in the number 2574, 5 represents 500 but the 7 represents 70. Many difficulties in arithmetic can be traced back to a child's lack of understanding of place value.

Reinforcement: In learning theory, reinforcement refers to the strengthening of a response or behaviour by some form of intrinsic or extrinsic reward.

Self-efficacy: The beliefs one has about one's own competency (or lack thereof) in various activities.

Self-talk: Inner language we use to guide or regulate our actions and thoughts. Self-talk can be valuable in the early stages of learning new skills and strategies.

Sight vocabulary: Words that are recognised immediately by sight.

Strategy: A mental plan of action.

Strategy training: The direct teaching and practice of mental plans of action that will help a learner attempt a particular task or problem efficiently.

Task-approach skills: These are the procedures a learner uses step by step as he or she works through a task efficiently. An effective strategy (mental plan of action) usually incorporates such task-approach skills to enable it to be implemented.

References

Adelson, R. (2004). Instruction versus exploration in science learning. *Monitor on Psychology, 35*, 6. Online at: http://www.apa.org/monitor/jun04/instruct.html

Allington, R. L. (2001). *What really matters for struggling readers?* New York: Longman.

Boaler, J. (1999). Mathematics for the moment, or the millennium? *Education Week, 18, 29*, 30–31.

Borich, G. D. (2007). *Effective teaching methods: Research-based practice* (6th ed.). Upper Saddle River, NJ: Merrill-Prentice Hall.

Boulware-Gooden, R., Carreker, S., Thornhill, A., & Joshi, R. M. (2007). Instruction in metacognitive strategies enhances reading comprehension and vocabulary achievement of Third-Grade students. *Reading Teacher, 61, 1*, 7–77.

Carnine, D. W., Silbert, J., Kameenui, E. J., Tarver, S. G., & Jongjohann, K. (2006). *Teaching struggling and at-risk readers: A direct instruction approach.* Upper Saddle River, NJ: Pearson-Merrill-Prentice Hall.

Clay, M. M. (1985). *The early detection of reading difficulties.* Auckland: Heinemann.

Coltheart, M., & Prior, M. (2006). Learning to read in Australia. *Australian Journal of Learning Disabilities, 11, 4*, 157–164.

Crozier, S. & Sileo, N. M. (2005). Encouraging positive behaviour with social stories. *Teaching Exceptional Children, 37, 6*, 26–31.

Davies, A., & Ritchie, D. (2004). *THRASS: Teaching Handwriting, Reading and Spelling Skills.* Chester: THRASS UK.

De Lemos, M. M. (2004). Effective strategies for the teaching of reading: What works, and why. In B. A. Knight & W. Scott (Eds.) *Learning difficulties: multiple perspectives* (pp.17–28). Frenchs Forest, NSW: Pearson Education Australia.

Dempsey, I., & Foreman, P. (2001). A review of educational approaches for individuals with autism. *International Journal of Disability, Development and Education, 48*, 103–16.

Dempster, F. N. (1991). Synthesis of research on reviews and tests. *Educational Leadership, 48, 7*, 71–76.

Department of Education, Science and Training (Australia). (2005). *Teaching Reading: National Inquiry into the Teaching of Literacy*, Canberra: Australian Government Publishing Service.

Dole, S. (2003). Applying psychological theory to helping students overcome learned difficulties in mathematics: an alternative approach to intervention. *School Psychology International, 24, 1,* 95–114.

Dorl, J. (2007). Think aloud! Increase your teaching power. *Young Children, 62, 4,* 101–105.

Farkota, R. (2005). Basic math problems: the brutal reality! *Bulletin: Learning Difficulties Australia, 37, 3,* 10–11.

Fountas, I. C.,& Pinnell, G. S. (2001). *Guiding readers and writers in Grades 3–6.* Portsmouth, NH: Heinemann.

Graham, S., & Harris, K.R. (2005). *Writing better: Effective strategies for teaching students with learning difficulties.* Baltimore: Brookes.

Greer, S. (2006). A study of the effect of calculator use on computational skills of high school students. In L.P. McCoy (Ed.) *Studies in teaching 2006: Research Digest* (pp. 61–66). Winston-Salem, NC: Wake Forest University.

Hardman, M. L., Drew, C. J., & Egan, W. W. (2005). *Human exceptionality: School, community, and family* (8th ed.). Boston: Pearson-Allyn & Bacon.

Hay, I., Elias, G., & Booker, G. (2005). Students with learning difficulties in relation to literacy and numeracy. *Schooling Issues Digest 2005/1.* Canberra: Australian Government Department of Education, Science and Training. Online at: http://dest.gov.au/schools/publications/digest.

Heller, K. W., & Bigge, J. L. (2005). Augmentative and alternative communication. In S. J. Best, K. W. Heller, & J. L. Bigge (Eds.) *Teaching individuals with physical or multiple disabilities* (5th ed.). Upper Saddle River, NJ: Pearson-Merrill-Prentice Hall.

Hetzroni, O. E., & Shrieber, B. (2004). Word processing as an assistive technology tool for enhancing academic outcomes of students with writing disabilities in the general classroom. *Journal of Learning Disabilities, 37, 2,* 143–54.

House of Commons Education and Skills Committee (Britain). (2005). *Teaching children to read.* London: TSO.

Howell, S., & Kemp, C. (2006). An international perspective of early number sense. *Australian Journal of Learning Disabilities, 11, 4,* 197–207.

Kauchak, D. & Eggen, P. (2007). *Learning and teaching: Research-based methods* (5th ed.). Boston: Allyn & Bacon.

Kelly, G. (2006). A check on Look, Cover, Write, Check. *Bulletin: Learning Difficulties Australia, 38, 1,* 6–7.

Kindsvatter, R., Wilen, W., & Ishler, M. (1992). *Dynamics of effective teaching* (2nd ed.). New York: Longman.

Kirschner, P. A., Sweller, J., & Clark, R. E. (2006). Why minimal guidance during instruction does not work: an analysis of the failure of constructivist, discovery, problem-based, experiential and inquiry-based teaching. *Educational Psychologist, 4, 2,* 75–86.

Lerner, J., & Kline, F. (2006). *Learning disabilities and related disorders* (10th ed.). Boston: Houghton Mifflin.

Lewis, R. B., & Doorlag, D. H. (2006). *Teaching special students in general education classrooms* (7th ed.). Upper Saddle River, NJ: Pearson-Merrill-Prentice Hall.

Lloyd, S., & Wernham, S. (1995). *Jolly Phonics*. Chigwell: Jolly Learning.

Lyndon, H. (1989). 'I did it my way': An introduction to Old Way–New Way. *Australasian Journal of Special Education, 13,* 32–7.

Massengill, D. (2006). Mission accomplished, it's learnable now: Voices of mature challenged spellers using a word study approach. *Journal of Adolescent and Adult Literacy, 49,* 5, 420–431.

Monroe, B. W. & Troia, G. A. (2006). Teaching writing strategies to middle school students with disabilities. *Journal of Educational Research, 100,* 1, 21–32.

Muter, V., & Snowling, C. (2004). *Early reading development and dyslexia*. London: Whurr.

National Council of Teachers of Mathematics (US). (2005). *Overview: Principles for school mathematics.* Online at: http://standards.nctm.org/document/chapter2/index.htm

National Council of Teachers of Mathematics (US). (2000). *Principles and standards for school mathematics.* Reston, VA: NCTM.

National Reading Panel (US). (2000). *Teaching children to read: An evidence-based assessment of the scientific research literature on reading and its implications for reading instruction.* Washington, DC: National Institute of Child Health and Human Development.

Nelson, B., & Sassi, A. (2007). What math teachers need most. *Education Digest, 72,* 6, 54–56.

Nichols, R. (1985). *Helping your child spell.* Earley: University of Reading.

Nicolini, M. B. (2006). Making thinking visible: Writing in the centre. *The Clearinghouse, 80,* 2, 66–69.

Nuthall, G. (2004). Relating classroom teaching to student learning: A critical analysis of why research has failed to bridge the theory-practice gap. *Harvard Education Review, 74,* 273–306.

O'Brien, C. (2005). Modifying learning strategies for classroom success. *Teaching exceptional children plus, 1,* 3 (n.p). Available online at: http://escholarship.bc.edu/education/tecplus/vol1/iss3/art3

Ormrod, J. (2000) *Educational psychology* (3rd ed.). Columbus: OH: Merrill.

Paas, F., Renkl, A., & Sweller, J. (2004). Cognitive load theory: Instructional implications of the interaction between information structures and cognitive architecture. *Instructional Science, 32,* 1–8.

Parker, M., & Hurry, J. (2007). Teachers' use of questioning and modelling comprehension skills in primary schools. *Educational Review, 59,* 3, 299–314.

Pierangelo, R., & Giuliani, G. (2006). *Learning disabilities: A practical approach to foundations, assessment, diagnosis and teaching.* Boston, MA: Pearson-Allyn & Bacon.

Polloway, E. A., Patton, J. R., & Serna, L. (2005). *Strategies for teaching learners with special needs* (8th ed.). Upper Saddle River, NJ: Merrill-Prentice Hall.

Poulter, M. (2002). Focus on spelling. *Literacy Today, 32,* 10–11.

Rose, J. (2005). *Independent review of the teaching of early reading: Interim report.* London: Department for Education and Skills.

Sewell, K. (2000). *Breakthroughs: How to reach students with autism.* Verona, WI: Attainment Company.

Sipe, L.R. (2001). Invention, convention and intervention: Invented spelling and the teacher's role. *Reading Teacher, 53, 3,* 264–273.

Swanson, H.L. (2000). What instruction works for students with learning disabilities? In R. Gersten, E. Schiller, & S. Vaughn (Eds.) *Contemporary special education research.* Mahwah, NJ: Erlbaum.

Timimi, S. (2006). A critique of the international consensus statement on ADHD. In Slife, B. (Ed.) *Taking Sides: Clashing views on psychological issues* (14th ed., pp. 210–213). Dubuque, IA: McGraw-Hill.

Tse, S. K., Lam, J. W., Lam R. Y. H, Loh, E. K. Y., & Westwood, P. S. (2007). Pedagogocal correlates of reading comprehension in English and Chinese. *L1 Educational Studies in Language and Literature, 7, 2,* 71–91.

Turnbull, A., Turnbull, R., & Wehmeyer, M. L. (2007). *Exceptional lives: Special education in today's schools* (5th ed.). Upper Saddle River, NJ: Pearson-Merrill-Prentice Hall.

Vukovic, R. K., & Siegel, L. S. (2006). The double-deficit hypothesis: a comprehensive analysis of the evidence. *Journal of Learning Disabilities, 39, 1,* 25–47.

Westwood, P. S., & Graham, L. (2000). How many children with special needs in regular classes? *Australian Journal of Learning Disabilities, 5, 3,* 24–35.

Wright, C. (2006). ADHD in the classroom. *Special Education Perspectives, 15, 2,* 3–8.

Xin, Y. P., Grasso, J. C., Dipipi-Hoy, C. M., & Jitendra, A. (2005). The effects of purchasing skill instruction for individuals with developmental disabilities: a meta-analysis. *Exceptional Children, 71, 4,* 379–400.

Index